RAINBOWS
— *in My* —
POCKET

*The Life and Times
of a Former Kid in
Small Town America*

ZED MERRILL

Order this book online at www.trafford.com
or email orders@trafford.com

Most Trafford titles are also available at major online book retailers.

Print information available on the last page.

ISBN: 978-1-4907-6297-5 (sc)
ISBN: 978-1-4907-6299-9 (hc)
ISBN: 978-1-4907-6298-2 (e)

Library of Congress Control Number: 2015912173

Trafford rev. 12/22/2015

 www.trafford.com

North America & international
toll-free: 1 888 232 4444 (USA & Canada)
fax: 812 355 4082

To the
unforgettable people
who made up
the colors
in my rainbow

*

CONTENTS

PROLOGUE

There were good times and there were bad times for some of those people I grew up with in Albany, Oregon. I'm thankful I wasn't touched by the bad times. Some of my friends were, but I never heard any of them complain. In fact, I never knew about the hardships a couple of them were going through until nearly seventy years later. Also, I didn't learn until many years after his death how my father quietly helped some of those families.

But I was touched by the friendship of these people and the good times we had together. All are gone now, except for two of us at this writing. And because of those friends, and some wonderful parents who guided me somehow miraculously unbruised throughout those innocent years, I can truthfully say, as I look back over my shoulder, I was blessed to have had rainbows in my pocket.

Zed Merrill

INTRODUCTION

Growing up as a kid during those times in a small town like Albany, Oregon, is an experience that might be difficult to describe to today's generation. But I'm willing to give it a try.

Those of you who know what it was like, whether you were from Maine, Illinois, or California, I'm sure you're going to see yourself somewhere in one of these stories. Maybe going deep for one of those back lot passes, racing a pal to kick the can in the middle of a street, or swinging from a ring for a swan dive into a lazy river.

We were never known as a "gang." I guess you could call us the "West Enders" and there were two age-level groups. The older guys, about five of them, were somewhere around fifteen years old; and the younger group of about seven, that included me, with ages that ranged from eleven to about fourteen.

And then there was the main guy who interacted with both groups. His name was Bob Pengra, and I always considered him the boss, the go-to guy, and probably the oldest by at least four years. I remember my dad telling me many years later that the parents felt Bob could always be trusted to look out for the younger ones. And he was.

By the way, from here on, I'll refer to the guys as the "guys" and individually by their last names. That's what you do back then. None of that kiddy first name stuff.

Also, I'll be calling my dad Pop because that's what he went by around the house. The nicknames he gave us kids were Snooky for my brother Frank, Snifter for sister Julia, and Nimble (short for nimble nip) for me.

And I think I should also mention that some of the names on the following pages have been changed for obvious reasons. I'm sure you will become keenly aware of these places when a particular event occurs.

CHAPTER 1

THE BIG APPLE *The great train rides, brother Frank's Indian Reservation, the scary lookalikes from upstairs, and membership into the West Enders.*

I was born during the Roaring Twenties, evolved into a kid riding my bike and playing street ball during the thirties, and then a teenager who hit the ground running at the beginning of the forties.

But before we get started, I want to mention that my first recollection of anything was not about growing up in the small town of Albany, Oregon. Yes, I was born there in 1926, and I do remember a couple of things, like riding a kiddy car and sticking a spoon in our dog's rear end, but it was being on a big train going somewhere when my memory kicked in. That somewhere would be the complete opposite of Albany. Like New York City, no less.

We arrived there in 1931 and it's where we lived for the next two years. Pop got a job that had something to do with the Keystone Utilities because of the depression and that his office was on Wall Street. When I say *we*, I mean my mom and Pop, my brother Frank, who was about eleven, and me somewhere around four. This didn't include my nine-year-old sister Julia who insisted on staying back in Albany awhile with Aunt Mary to take care of our dog Scotty. How she got away with that I'll never know.

I need to add here this was not a permanent move. Pop was somehow granted a leave-of-absence from his position with Mountain States Power Company to do what he was hired away to do. I can't believe it would take two years.

We lived in a tall apartment building up in Mt. Vernon, north of the Bronx. I remember it had a lot of trees around it and a fenced-off play area for kids that was supervised by a couple of white-uniformed women that I guess were babysitters but looked

1

more like prison guards to me. Like I said, I was only four when we arrived there, but I can remember vividly today the layout of the rooms, even a couple of the pictures on the wall.

We were only there a couple of months when my grandma, Pop's mom, passed away back in Albany. Now listen to this: Pop was given the time off, took a train all the way back to Albany, packed Julia for the return trip, and stopped off in Wisconsin to bury Grandma. Pop and Julia then continued east by train to New York. My sister doesn't recall how long this adventure took, only that she had a a compartment of her own and was a favorite of the porters.

Living in the penthouse of our apartment were twin girls whose parents were becoming world famous entertainers.

I remember playing often with them in the outdoor play area, and I'll never forget what they looked like. I had never seen twins before, especially up close, and these two were as homely as they get. Even at four I could see that. Obviously, their last names won't be mentioned here, especially when you read following:

Julia also became friends with them and since they were more near her age, they often played together. Julia remembers after several weeks had passed when there was a knock on our door and she happened to answer it. Standing there were the twins, side by side, and one of them got right to the point.

"Our mother says we can't play with you anymore because you're an Indian."

With that said, they turned and walked down the hallway and took the elevator up to their penthouse.

It didn't take much of an investigation on my mom's part to uncover what brought this all about. My brother Frank had been telling some of his wide-eyed New York classmates that since they considered him a Wild West inhabitant of the far off Indian country of Oregon, he might as well play along with them. He told them, in all seriousness, that he was part Indian and we had all lived on a reservation before coming to New York. Needless to say, my mom quickly set the record straight on that one too.

In the early part of 1932, Pop was offered a permanent position in Wall Street, but decided living in the big city is not what he and Mom wanted for their family. When that was made known to the Board of Directors at Mountain States Power back in Albany, Pop was offered the vice presidency of the company. We were all soon on the train heading back out west and anxious to get back on the reservation. A few years later, Pop was made president of Mountain States, then when the company merged with Pacific Power & Light in Portland he became chairman of the board. But he and Mom would remain in Albany.

Getting back to the early 1930s, I remember we quickly moved from our house near the center of town farther west up to West Elm and Sixth Street. And it would all start a couple of months later when I entered the first grade and was escorted to the opposite side of the block to Seventh Street to Maple School by my mom and new friends Billy Ewing and Tommy Dawson.

I was now a new member of the West enders.

Chapter 1

1927. Waiting for life to get underway. Sister Julia, me in the middle, and brother Frank

Being from the Wild West I might as well play the part.

My reaction to having to move to New York City. Wherever that is.

Me on the left with Darrell McClain, my first pal from the west end

With my dad and mom and ready for my first day in school. How I hated that hat.

CHAPTER 2

OUR TOWN *The Rialto Olympics, Spring Hill time, escape from Chinatown, stars in our eyes, and the national record nobody wanted to talk about.*

Before we go much further, it might be a good idea to roll out the map and tell you where we're going to be spending the following time together. Look up in the far left corner and you'll see the state of Oregon. That's where we're going to be. No, it's not pronounced Ore-gone! It's Ore-gun!

The small town in Oregon I was blessed with being brought up in was Albany, population then somewhere around 6,000. Today it's more like 52,000. We had a courthouse with the typical large clock tower, but it was torn down about 1939 and replaced with an imposing structure that still stands to this day in the middle third street facing down Broadalbin toward the heart of downtown. I can remember the big attraction when it was built was the installation of the town's first self-operated elevator, or the first ever anywhere as far as we were concerned. It would attract the curious, especially on Saturdays. People would get in line for a free demonstration ride up and down to the second floor.

Exciting! But then we were in the fast-moving modern era of talking pictures and the Sunday newspaper adventures of Buck Rogers and Flash Gordon, so anything was possible.

Oh yes, before we continue on, Albany sits in the heart of the Willamette Valley about sixty-eight miles south of Portland and about a mile west just off of today's I-5 Freeway.

The old two-lane highway no longer runs down through main street, which may have been the scene of an encounter some of us kids had with a world famous movie star. At least we want to believe we did. We'll go there a page or so later.

5

I remember I wasn't in school very long when my new friend Billy Ewing, who lived right across the street from Maple School, had just entered the second grade ahead of me when he suddenly came down with scarlet fever. I don't remember how long he was out of school but I do know he came close to dying. And since he missed all of the first grade, he was forced to start the grade over again. That put him in the danger zone, which was the desk right across from me.

This was the beginning of the era where I grew up with a lot of great pals, swam in the dirty Calapooia River, played touch tackle football up on Seventh Street, and rode a bike, which, by the way, never *ever* crossed Railroad Street into the no-man's land of the dreaded tough East End.

To this very day, and this is the honest truth, there are parts of that East End I've never seen. And for a very good reason. Tuffy Logan may still be there lurking in the shadows, ready to jump out and scare the crap out of me. At a great risk, we'll visit there later.

On Main Street we had three theaters, all on the north side of the street. The Venetian and Granada were in one block in the middle of town, and the Rialto was one block east. The Venetian, which was the town's classiest theater (it had a balcony) showed only first run movies, usually the kissy-kissy stuff and then once in a while the awesome shoot 'em up James Cagney gangster films. On Saturday mornings, we were blessed with a live on-stage Mickey Mouse Club. I mean the original Mickey Mouse Club. The theater was always packed with kids. Some guy would play the organ and we would all sing the words flashed up on the screen.

This was usually the cue for a couple of us to make up our own hilarious lyrics which were stupid and often got the shaking no-no finger from the usherette.

They had on-stage contests, gave away prizes, and then showed Mickey Mouse cartoons and a serial. On the way out, you were given a free ice cream Dixie cup at the door. Everything for the price of a dime. Was life good or what!?

The Walt Disney people also published in the early1930s a Mickey Mouse magazine, and for my eighth birthday I was given a one-year subscription. I remember not long afterward, I entered the magazine's "Didga Contest," where you were encouraged to think up and enter your own "Didga ever . . ." slogan.

For example: "Didga ever see a cream puff?" or "Didga ever see a board walk?" I knew I had a winner, so I sent in "Didga ever see Max Baer?" For those of you who haven't a clue, Max Baer was the world heavyweight boxing champion.

Well, my Aunt Mary went into shock because the line suggests have you seen Max *naked*? It was too late because the mail had already gone, much to the amusement of my parents and brother and sister. My mom said, "Don't worry. He's not going to win anyway."

Two weeks later I got a letter and a package from Disney Studios congratulating me as the second place winner.

In the package with the letter was a Mickey Mouse watch, a bright red and white Mickey Mouse sweatshirt, and a two-year subscription to the magazine. Plus, a story in an upcoming issue of the magazine about winning second place. As far as Aunt Mary was concerned, I had won for pornography and we'll never speak of it again.

Now back to downtown.

A few doors away in the middle of the block on First Street was the Granada, a kid's heaven of shoot-'em-up-cowboy double features, serials, cartoons and comedies. This was our escape into the world where a fast-riding, quick-shooting Tim McCoy and Ken Maynard always got the bad guy and usually kissed his horse instead of the girl. Sometimes they would show a cops-and-robber movie where the crook would always get shot or thrown in the big house, or one about an airmail pilot, most always Pat O'Brien, who would survive a crash but his sidekick wouldn't.

Then there were the scary moments when some of us would jump out of our seats and run for our lives. Not from what was happening up on the screen but from what was darting here and there beneath the seats. We called them the gangster rats.

But the one main concern for the parents of the kids flocking to the Granada on Saturday afternoons, and Saturday nights especially, was the general location of the Granada. On each side of the theater was a huge tavern, and the big brawls that would go on inside would sometimes spill over onto the kid's bike stalls in front of the theater. Most of these were often more exciting than what we saw up on the screen.

Your folks either dropped you off by car right in front of the Granada or told you to run as fast as you could across main street to and from the protective custody of the front of the Blain Clothing store. An eleven-year-old kid dodging cars going in both directions and risking serious injury was the sound parental advice you had to obey in order to avoid being within a few feet of the dreadful influence of one of the two rowdy saloons.

Then a whole block and a half east was the Rialto.

This is where most of the musicals played, and for some reason this is where you went on Sundays. You could always count on seeing Bob Hope, Bing Crosby, and Dorothy Lamour. But the theater was tiny. The aisles on both sides of the center seats were only two seats wide; and if you sat in the center of the back row, you had to scoot down a little so as not to get the projector light in the back of your head. A former usherette once told me there were only sixty-two seats in the theater. That may have been stretching it a few.

This is where the world famous Rialto Olympics were held, so named by our leader Bob Pengra. The event was usually conducted under the cover of night, and the darker the better. The Olympics got its start some time around when I was about twelve and was usually held on a Saturday night.

Here were the rules of the game:

Four of us would gather down across the street in front of the teen hangout, The Cravemore Café, some time around 9:15, all the while keeping an eye on the front of the Rialto. It was always this time of the evening when Dick Henderson, the son the owner, would dismiss the gal in the ticket booth and step outside to wait for any latecomers for the second show. One of us would count to fifty and then this is when we would strike.

Somebody would toss a coin to see who was "it," and "it" meant he had to go into The Cravemore, ask a waitress if he could use the phone in back to call his parents under the pretense to come and pick him up.

Instead, the "it" guy would call the Rialto. We could hear the theater phone ringing from across the street, see Dick Henderson turn and go inside, and then knowing it would take him a couple of minutes to climb the narrow stairs up to the theater's tiny office and answer the phone, we would then make our dash for the Rialto.

It had to be perfectly timed because it was about sixty-five yards away. Some of the guys would wear their tennis shoes just for this event.

Once we reached the theater, we quickly and quietly slipped through the door single file, then the teeny little lobby, and as we heard a voice off in the distance above somewhere saying . . . "hello? . . . hello? . . . we were in the darkness of the theater by then slipping into and slumping down in our seats. We had crossed the finish line as winners once again.

The "it" guy? Well, he had to make his dash alone.

And if he knew he wasn't going to make it, he would peel off and work his way back across the street in between a couple of parked cars to the protective custody of The Cravemore. If he had to do this he would miss the second show, get on his bike parked in the alley back of The Cravemore, and pedal home alone in the dark. However, since the "it" guy usually didn't make it safely across the finish line, our rules considerate to the point he was exempt from the coin toss the next time.

The same lone usherette on duty always witnessed the event but never squealed because her boyfriend's little brother was one of the dashers. In the half dozen or so Rialto Olympics I was involved in, not once did we lose. I only had to be the "it" guy twice; one of those times I completed the dash without getting caught and the other time I didn't stand a chance.

I remember one time Ewing was "it" and he ran smack into Dick Henderson before he even reached the lobby. Out of breath, and soaked from a heavy rain, he breathlessly explained to Dick under a head-lock that he was there to pick up his sister. That might have worked only Dick said, "You don't have a sister, Billy!"

Crime doesn't pay when you live in a small town.

In the heart of downtown was the bridge that spanned the Willamette River leading north to the rolling hills of lush farm land we called North Albany. The highway, coming off the bridge, followed the river eight miles west to Corvallis and then curved its way through the coast range to the shores of the Pacific.

As you immediately come off the bridge, you make a right turn, passing the golf course on the right, then on up through Hogtown (we'll stop there in a moment), and two miles later you turn right again on Nebergal Loop Road and around the next curve you'll be at the foot of the house my folks had built in 1936. This is just south of the Spring Hill area and a place I would call home until I left for the service in 1944.

But during those eight years in the country, and thanking God for the life-saving invention of the bicycle, I would never actually leave the west side of Albany.

Getting back to the bridge. Some of my memories of that steel and concrete structure was seeing kids walk across the cement railing from one side to the other with their hands outstretched like balancing on a circus high wire. I just now got a cold chill.

Underneath, on the North Albany side, was the town's floating swimming pool that set in the water tied up near the riverbank. Next to it was a huge slide that I swear was five stories tall. The pool is where I learned to swim as an eight-year-old when Bruce Dowling, the lifeguard, threw me into the deep end of the pool and yelled, "Swim, little Merrill!" I did. Floodwaters in the late thirties would wipe out the pool and slide.

Underneath the bridge, as you entered town, and located along the railroad tracks near the river was the Saturday entertainment center. The auction house. Being basically a farm community, farmers came from miles around to auction off, or buy cattle, housewares, or whatever. It was like going to the State Fair every week. It was a swirling activity of people noises, all mixed in with the smell of hotdogs and hamburgers being cooked in onions and complimented with the distinct aroma of fresh cow pies.

Then there was the rapid language of the auctioneer, Dan Roth, that only the farmers understood. I can remember one time seeing a farm girl with a basket of six puppies she was selling for a dime each. By noon she had sold them all, obviously to some kid who spent his movie money for the puppy, not thinking, of course, what his or her, mother would say about another mouth to feed during those difficult times. To a kid, it was an exciting place to be on Saturday mornings before you ventured up one block to main street, lined up in front of Blains, and made your dash across traffic to the Granada.

The one incident that sticks in my mind about the bridge involved the sign. It was mounted over the entrance of the structure coming into town from North Albany.

It read: "Welcome to Albany, the Friendly City."

One day, while going to town with Pop, and as we approached the bridge, we looked up at the sign, which was a good thirty feet high over the entrance, and it had several empty whisky bottles tied with colored string dangling from it. The next day they were gone. Then the following day, they were back up on the sign and down they came again. An article ran in the daily paper condemning the action to hooligans who were showing no respect for their town. When the light of morning appeared the next day, there they were once more. Only this time two extra bottles were added to the display, plus more festive red and white paper streamers and, of all things, a plucked corpse of a chicken hanging from a noose. My kind of town Albany is.

The bridge entered Main Street and continued south becoming Ellsworth Street. To your left, Main Street went on for another three blocks housing several retail stores on each side that included the Rialto Theater and The Cravemore. Among those was Woolworth's Five and Dime, Ben Franklin's, Jack Cathy's Men's Store, Nedry's Red Top with their fifteen-cent flamethrower chili, and Sam Frager's Furniture Store where almost everybody in town went to buy their furniture.

Next to Sam was his secondhand store, across the street was a service station and two blocks farther down was the Ellsworth Apartments where I swear everyone lived at one time or another. Among the many was my mom and Pop when they first came to Albany in the mid 1920s, my sister Julia and her husband Pete during the early 1940s, and then Norma and I right after the war in 1946.

Right across the street on the north side was Roy's Hamburgers, a four-seat counter diner where Roy personally created no-two-alike burger sensations for a dime. He was still there a couple years after the war where I'm afraid his burger fame became his undoing. He raised his price to twenty-five cents.

But just half a block west of Roy's toward downtown was a mysterious Chinese Café located in the even more mysterious Imperial Hotel. As a kid, I never heard of anyone ever eating Chinese food in Albany. To me this only happened in Charlie Chan detective murder movies at the Granada where some bad guy usually croaked to death on bamboo shoots. I was forbidden to stay off that side of the block because of what went on upstairs in the Imperial Hotel. Well, actually my folks never told me what was going on up there but the older guys certainly did.

Then one Saturday evening, after being inspired, or scared spitless by one of those Chinatown murder epics at the Granada, our circle of guys, the oldest probably being thirteen and the youngest eleven, ventured cautiously up the street toward the forbidden Imperial Hotel. My mouth felt like it had sand in it and I'm sure my eyes looked as big as hub caps. The big challenge was on!

One of our guys opened the door going up the narrow dark stairway to the rooms up above, and I remember thinking how on earth did I get second in line with that wobbly legged, horrified mess of adolescence. Half way up the stairs a buzzer sounded. The lead guy had stepped on a button hidden under the stair's carpet. For one frightening, paralyzing moment, nobody moved. We were suddenly frozen in silence, and I remember wishing I was home right then laying on the rug with my head propped up on the side of my sleeping dog, safe and sound, listening to the Fred Allen Show.

"What in hell do you kids want?" It was a woman's low pitched voice coming from behind us down the stairs. Then a door suddenly opened on the stairs above and down stepped a heavyset Chinaman. The first one I ever saw in Albany, and this guy wasn't Charlie Chan. How five us got down those stairs so fast, nearly bowling over the woman, and across the street and racing into the pitch darkness to hide behind the Ellsworth Apartments escapes my memory even to this day.

Proven evidence that fear can accomplish anything.

Sometime later I was with my mom in the Grocerveteria, the large downtown grocery store on second street, when a woman walked past me out of range of my mom and said softly with a slight smile, "How you doing, sweetie?" I'm sure my mom wondered on the way home why I was suddenly so quiet, which was something unheard of in the Merrill household.

As I said before: fear can accomplish anything.

Back standing now at the foot of the bridge looking to your right down Main Street, the heart of downtown stretches out for four blocks. The Granada and Venetian theaters with the saloons on the north side of the first block to your right, and across the street on the south side, as I remember, was Hurley's Drug Store on the east corner, Tripp & Tripp Realtors, a bakery, Blain Clothing, Jenk's Variety Store (we called it Jenks Junk Store) and Long's Shoe Store on the west corner. Payless Drugs would come along many years later to replace Jenks.

Across from Long's on Broadalbin Street was the First National Bank Building, the town's six-story skyscraper, challenged only by the six-story Albany Hotel located a few blocks east over on Second Street. As a kid I never liked going into the bank building because on the top floors is where all the evil dentists lurked with their deadly pain machines. For some sinister reason, I was always thrust into the chair from hell operated by Dr. Turner. He added to his arsenal of nightmares a bad case of foul breath, which on a number of occasions was substituted with a knock-over aroma of Jim Beam.

It was also rumored that while he was under the influence one evening, Doc Turner got an equally loaded prominent Albany businessman in the chair and was able to pull almost all his teeth when only one pull would have been necessary.

Moving west on First Street from the bank building were a number of stores of which I can remember only a few. Let's see, there was JC Penny's in the middle of the north side of the street, the Union Telegraph store, a woman's apparel shop on the corner, and Floyd Mullen's Feed & Seed on the opposite west end of the block. The only ones I can remember located across the street on the south side was a fabric shop, Warner's Hardware, French's Jewelry with their landmark big clock towering about twenty feet above the sidewalk, and the Sunnybrook Café.

Later, in the fall of 1944, I would buy Norma her engagement ring at French's and it cost me an eye-popping $100.

My Model A was parked right in front of the store and and it was there I slipped it on her finger. Now was I cool or what!?

The last block on Main Street consisted of the St. Francis Hotel, the liquor store, a couple of great secondhand stores, a paint and body shop, the big building that housed the Order of the Mason's, and a corner service station. This is where US Highway 99E made its turn and headed east down Main Street. The highway in those days made its way up from the south from Eugene through Albany's west end residential area, through the middle of downtown and out the other end going east through that residential area and finally heading north about a mile later to Salem and Portland. Today, the I-5 freeway bypasses downtown a couple of miles to the east.

It was on that corner service station where the highway turns east and becomes the main drag that I'm positive the three of us saw stars before our eyes. Or at least one. I remember exactly what the three of us were doing at the time. Keep in mind this was in 1937.

McClain and I were checking the air in our bike's tires and Ewing was getting an Orange Crush out of the cooler by the service station door when this sedan pulls up for gas. A man and a woman and a girl about our age climbed out of the car to stretch their legs and began a conversation with the guy pumping gas. Ewing then comes over to where we were and in his excitement can hardly get his words out.

"Guess who I just said hello to?" he stammers, which he often did when he got excited. "Shirley Temple!" he blurted out before McClain and I could say anything.

I remember seeing the girl had curly blond hair tucked under a tan cap, a blue-type dress and Mary Jane shoes with tan socks. She smiled in our direction, then turned away to talk to the older woman, who was obviously her mother. It was then that McClain, who was usually the most brazen of all the guys, walked over to her and the older couple. What the dickens was he doing!? What if it was Shirley Temple? Naw, it can't be. This is Albany, Oregon, and why is she riding in a car and not on a train? Keep in mind airlines didn't really exist much then.

Now McClain is being approached by a guy from a car that had pulled in behind. McClain is a dead man. I wanted to get on my bike and get out of there but I was paralyzed. The girl, McClain, and the others by the car started laughing and then he walked back to Ewing and me with a big grin on his face.

"Yeah, that's Shirley Temple," he says, "If we're going to the show we better get going." His exact words.

With that said we got on our bikes and left. McClain, being the practical joker he was, insisted it was her, but I was beginning to believe it wasn't. Ewing was starting to fade in his discovery and by the time the show was over he told McClain, in no uncertain terms, he was making it all up. She wasn't Shirley Temple. Period! The girl and the adults had obviously told McClain that she wasn't the famous movie star and they were getting a laugh over it.

Several years later, I asked McClain about the encounter and he just smiled, shrugged, and said, "Believe what you want." Which was typical of him. Ewing changed his mind and started believing it was the movie star and that McClain was telling us the truth. I wasn't so sure.

Now let's fast speed ahead seventy-four years to 2010.

I'm reading a book written by Shirley Temple when I came to a passage that made my chin drop. She writes about how her parents decided in 1937, when she was the world's number one box office attraction, that she needed a vacation away from Hollywood. The plan was that she and her parents would drive up north through Oregon and Washington to Vancouver, B.C., stay about a week, and then turn around and make the long drive back. This meant driving on Highway 99E that went right through downtown Albany. Also on the trip, following behind in another car, was the movie star's personal manager. This would explain the second car pulling into the service station and the driver approaching McClain.

So maybe McClain was right. Then I got to thinking: This is also the same kid who told me when I was four years old that Mickey Mouse had died, and I sat down on the sidewalk and cried.

When Norma and I were on our way to a cruise out of Miami back in the '80s we stopped off and visited McClain who was living nearby. He told us the Shirley Temple encounter was really true. He said her parents had asked him to tell us guys not to make a fuss over Shirley being there because they didn't want to attract attention to her. And the reason they were laughing was because McClain told them that he had a Shirley Temple doll and he played with it all the time. Typical McClain.

Heading back east now through town on the Second Street was the Linn Creamery, then a corner spot that would eventually become in later years Barrett's Sporting Goods. Down another block on the left was a shoe repair store, Taylor's Print Shop, the Grocerveteria (everybody's big grocery store), and Hamilton's Department Store on the corner. Across the street from all this, going in the same direction, west to east, was the Fire Department, City Hall, the Police Department, and Stiff's Furniture Store on the corner.

In the next block across the street on the south side of Second Street is the post office, then the drive- through Greyhound Bus Depot, which was home to Jim Christie's Greyhound Tavern, and Kurtz Grocery Store on the corner. Walking west to east across the street from the post office is the U. S. National Bank building, a savings and loan company (a sporting goods store run by Vince Barrett would eventually happen here) and on the corner, I can't remember what, but it would eventually become the site for The Hub Restaurant, the town's largest eating and meeting establishment.

Next block down on the north side was the Chevrolet dealership, which actually faced Ellsworth Street. Back in the thirties, it was always a major town event when the new cars would arrive on the back of those double-decker vehicle carriers. Townspeople would arrive, as well as those from the country, and every kid who had a bike would line them up across the street to witness the big gala unloading ceremony. As kids, we would pretend and argue over which Chevrolet was ours.

Farther down the same block from the dealership was the Albany Feed & Seed Store. A large, two-story ornate building that is now home to the impressive Albany Regional Museum. Sometime before the turn of the century, the big structure had been moved from several blocks away to its current location by means of many horses, rolling logs, and what-have-you. I can't fathom how they did it without wiping out a few merchants along the way and settling for a permanent I-give-up location in the middle of Second Street.

Across Second Street, still going west to east, I can only remember the telephone company and the north entrance to the Albany Hotel. This is where Lyons Street went north and south; and farther east on Second Street is where Frager's had a secondhand store, then the Owl Café sandwiched in there somewhere, followed by an auto and tire shop, then eventually Donahue's Auto Repair. From there east, the area faded into a residential district. The entrance to no-man's-land.

On Third Street, starting on Lyons Street and going back east to west, businesses began to disappear. Most notable along a three block stretch was Blaylock's grocery store, Mountain States Power Company, which was the head office for a service area that stretched throughout the Willamette Valley and northern Oregon coast over to the Idaho panhandle, then into northwest Montana, and most of Wyoming. Not many local people knew that.

Then came Irving's Garage where you could buy your Buick or Pontiac. After that, a couple of churches, an insurance company, the infamous Moose Lodge Dance Hall and, on a side street, the public library. My Aunt Mary first took me to the library one Saturday morning when I was about nine and said she was going to introduce me to Tom Sawyer. I was disappointed when I saw it was a book.

And sitting in the middle of Fourth Street, facing toward downtown, is the Linn County Court House, which was considered by most everyone living in Albany at the time as one of the community's finest buildings. I believe it still is.

A few blocks from downtown over on upper Lyons Street was the massive Armory building, where not only the local National Guard was stationed but where the big name dance bands of the thirties and forties entertained. Across the street was the American Legion Hall, which at one time was the Oregon Electric train station.

When the local WWI American Legionaries took over the building in the mid '30s, they placed a huge artillery cannon out front that quickly became a prime climbing target for every kid in town, including me. I remember seeing one little guy scoot up to the end of the barrel, wave to us below and then slip head first to the cement below. He quietly got up, cupped his bloody nose in his left hand and slowly walked away going east down the sidewalk. Not a cry or even a whimper. The rest of us froze. He was obviously one of the tough East Enders and lived somewhere beyond the Railroad Street border line that led into no man's land.

Over a couple of blocks more was the old jailhouse that sat directly across the First Presbyterian Church and located on what is now the backside of the courthouse. It also faced the other direction where Takena Park was once located. This block-size downtown park catered to kids splashing around in wading pools and families sitting on blankets during warm summer evenings enjoying the live band concerts.

It was said that one evening an inmate in the upstairs jailhouse across the street sent a message somehow over to the conductor requesting a specific tune. It was played. The prisoners never had it so good.

The jailhouse would also become the scene of every kid's Saturday matinee come true at the Granada. It was the big jailhouse shootout. As I remember, it happened sometime during the mid 1930s, and there were three of us who got a taste of what it must have been like. I'm not kidding. That's in a chapter coming up.

Albany also had a small college that became famous for its football teams whose record during the thirties had achieved national recognition. A record, I'm afraid, the town would just as soon everybody forgot about. The Pirates, as they were called, lost every game for something like eight straight years.

The college finally closed its doors near the end of the decade, not because of the losing streak, but because of the depression taking its toll. Supported by the Presbyterian Church, the school moved north to Portland to become Lewis and Clark College, but not before the football team finally broke its famous losing streak by tying Pacific University of Forest Grove, Oregon 6-6 in a fog-shrouded night game in Albany.

If my memory is correct, Pacific scored first. Then an Albany player later ran unseen across the goal line to tie the score. It wasn't because of his deceptive running talent, or his great teammate blocking, but rather from an assist from mother nature. The fog was so thick nobody saw him make the touchdown. Anyway, that's what some fans claimed.

This created a mystery indeed. In light of the team's inability to win anything over a period of something like sixty games, the townspeople wondered aloud over Monday morning coffee if the ball carrier, even if he could see through the fog, knew in which direction a goal line might be located, or if he could recognize it when he saw it.

I was at the game with Pengra and Ewing that night somewhere along the sidelines. I remember it was a wild and crazy atmosphere. You would have thought, instead of being a tie game, that the Pirates had actually won.

Personally, the historic event did have an effect on me because my big brother Frank played right guard for those amazing, record-breaking Albany Pirates.

Chapter 2

Me on the left with Billy Ewing and and Old Scotty. Shortly after this was taken, Ewing came down with scarlet fever.

Main Street looking west from the corner of Lyons Street. Taken in the late 1920s and looking the same in the mid 1930s

All suited up and ready for some tough action. Albany College could have used me during the 1930s.

First week in the second grade at Maple School. I was the first of about thirty kids who saddled up for the camera that day.

The downtown bridge crossing the Willamette River to North Albany. Here hung the infamous signs of the times.

Early members of the West Enders. Me on the left with that dumb hat again, Billy Ewing and Tommy Dawson.

CHAPTER 3

SEVENTH STREET. *Where touch football ruled, Clarence the parrot was to be avoided at all costs, kick the can was a serious boy/girl event, and the last of one-punch T. B. Lawford.*

In a west-end section of Seventh Street lies a block-long field of pavement between Elm and Maple Streets that a bunch of us guys during the 1930s staged some of the most awesome and heroic touch tackle football games in the history of the sport.

Let's begin with the 1935 season. The players ranged in age from seven to twelve and would number anywhere from six to eight, which depended on whether seven-year-old Donnie Eastburn could sneak past his mom to get out on the street, and if ten-year-old Billy Cochrane could convince his grandma he wouldn't get hurt, which he usually did. I was next to the youngest at nine. The others were Carlton Eastburn, Bill Ewing, T. B. Lawford (T. B. for tiny butt), Darrell McClain, George Tycer, and our fearless leader Bob Pengra, who had to be around thirteen years old.

On the rare occasion we would need an emergency substitution, which was usually due to one of us being kept home because of some infraction of a family disciplinary rule, we would give in to the unthinkable of evening up the sides by bringing in a girl from the sidelines over by the curb. Not just any girl, mind you. She was big Donna "The Buffalo" Marshall. She couldn't catch the ball if you handed it to her, but she could certainly block for the quarterback by intimidating the rushing defenders by sneering and just standing in their way. Her intimidation was that she was tall, fat, and had big boobs for a twelve year old. She also sweated a lot and that was when she wasn't playing. I remember the following year, after one particular early season game, her mother arrived on the scene and put a stop to "The Buffalo's" playing days. She penalized a couple of the older guys for a little too much holding. Especially in the huddles.

There were the usual hazards for using a paved street for a football field. One being, of course, was the pavement. There was no tackling and the way you stopped a ball carrier was touching him below the waist. Needless to say, we were all exuberate in our effort to make a real game out of it, so some of the touch-tackling and above-the-waist blocking would turn a little physical. The results were often a lot of skinned knees, twisted ankles, and torn clothes.

One sideline obstacle that could be counted on to cause some pain was a permanent "slow school" sign near the curb that marked one of our goal lines. I raced to that very spot once to leap in the air for one of Pengra's passes when the whole world exploded in my head. When I woke up everybody was standing over me and in the middle of all this confusion, I heard Eastburn yell, "He's dead, I just know it. Call an ambulance! Crap! And in front of my house too!"

After Doc Woodworth, at the nearby hospital, put a couple of stitches in my ear, Pop took me and some of the guys up to Brunskill's mom and pop grocery store for some root beer. Now in case you're wondering how a bunch of kids could pass that one up you needn't do so. We had already renamed the store Numbskulls.

One of the minor distractions, sometimes hilarious, bordering the goal line near the curb at Seventh and Maple Streets was a character named Clarence. He sat in a cage on the front porch of the Williams' house with an unobstructed view of what went on at the end of the street. If you guessed Clarence was a parrot, you're right.

One thing Clarence was good at was whistling. You know, the shrieking kind. And when the football action in front of Clarence became hectic, he became excited, started swaying back and forth, and whistling loud enough to disturb every living creature within six blocks. I'm serious. My Aunt Mary lived two blocks away and she could hear Clarence when she was vacuuming. She also knew it meant somebody was scoring six points.

Something had to be done about Clarence. And one of us sneaking up on the Williams' porch and teaching the bird to say other things, rather than letting out an irritating shriek, wasn't the answer. He would still let out that annoying whistle, but now he would follow up with "Go jump in the lake, idiot!" I admit this was fall-down funny to all of us, but not to Mr. Williams. After Clarence yelled this a couple times, and then followed up with "(whistle!) your mother wears army boots!", Mr. Williams had enough. His complaint circulated through our parents and each of us was given a good talking to by a dad or mom who had difficulty in keeping a straight face. Each of us promised Mr. Williams we would ignore Clarence while he untrained the parrot's vocabulary. And we did. At least we told each other we did.

It wasn't long afterward that Mrs. Attermont, who lived a couple houses away, walked up on the porch to visit Mrs. Williams when Clarence greeted her loud enough to frighten all the birds in the trees.

"(whistle!) Hey, toots! You're full of #&ZX!"

All I can remember is that Mr. Williams moved Clarence and his cage around to the back of the house and we never heard from the bird again. Except for a faraway whistle now and then. I don't think our parents were told about Clarence's cussing incident because none of us mentioned ever being called on the family carpet.

In later years, at a high school class reunion, one of our guys thought that an Albany College student walking by the Williams house taught Clarence Mrs. Attermont's famous greeting. A greeting, I was told, that took Mr. Williams a long time to get the parrot to forget about.

Playing kick the can, especially in the summer evening hours, was an event that made growing up on a neighborhood street during the 1930s a time in life that was especially golden. If some of you don't know the rules of the game, which resembles hide-and-seek in a way or if you haven't a clue what in the devil I'm talking about, then this is how it goes:

An empty can, the regular size that probably once held pork & beans, is set in the middle of the street. In this case in front of Eastburn's house, which was near the middle of the block. By pulling straws, the one who got the shortest was "it." This meant that he, or she, covered their eyes, put one foot on the can, and counted out loud to ten while the others all ran like crazy to hide behind houses, wood piles, bushes, cars in driveways, and behind large-trunk trees. The "it" person would then yell "here I come, ready or not" and then would suddenly experience a harsh feeling of loneliness while standing alone in the middle of an empty street where once seven to eight jabbering kids once stood. All was quiet. Except maybe for a faint faraway snicker or two.

"It" would then sneak around trying to spot someone, and if he did, he would then get in a foot race with the hider to beat him to the can by jumping over it and count him as being captured. But if the hider was faster he would beat "it" to the can and kick the Holey Moses out of it clear across the street and into Ewing's back- yard. The hider would then escape back across the street into the hiding places among the rest of the players, and "it" would start over again by placing the badly bent can in the middle of Seventh Street. If you're still with me, the object of the game is for the "it" person to capture all the hiders. If you're little Shelly Hobbs, you never won.

By the way, never attempt to play this game barefooted. And seriously, the real benefits of playing Kick the Can, especially for the guys who are now twelve years or older, was not whether you could beat "it" back to the can or not, but whether you could find the cutest girl to hide with. This meant a certain amount of snuggling together; and if you were a confident man-of-the-world type, maybe a giggling missing-the-mark kiss on the cheek.

I can remember quite vividly the warm summer evening when the Seventh Street Kick the Can event came to a halt, at least for our generation. One of the girls, who would often infiltrate our domain from a distant neighborhood toward the middle of town, complained directly to her lawyer father that one particular young man from our Seventh Street group had attempted to take a step beyond the kissy-giggle stage. This never reached our parents and the lawyer-father never intended it to, knowing that just his presence before us, standing in front of the headlights of his car, would strike holy fear through our souls. All of us, including the guilty guy, had seen enough of lawyers up on the movie screen sending guys like Cagney and Bogart to the electric chair.

Kick the Can made a comeback the following summer. Only this time it was usually supervised by somebody's mom in a rocking chair sitting on a centrally located porch in the neighborhood where she could keep a lookout for anything giggly going on. I especially remember this arrangement because more times than not, there would be somebody else's mom, or maybe Grandma, on a porch across the street, and a two-way, sometimes three-way conversation would be going on between them. In those days, only Buck Rogers and Flash Gordon had something that resembled a cell phone.

T. B. Langford's tenure in the neighborhood games was short-lived. He was a new apartment move-in down Maple Street which only lasted maybe about three months before his parents packed up and left for Salem. He was a cry baby type, always wanted to punch it out and knew cuss words I'd never heard before.

One day T. B. screamed something nasty at me during one touch tackle game and that did it. I recall calling timeout and marching across the street with both fists clenched ready to punch his T. B. (Tiny Butt) to the pavement. All of a sudden I was dropped like a sack of rocks. Fireworks started going off in my head in all directions.

I got up and staggered into a run for home which was down the street and around the corner and up to the end house on the block. All I remember was I kept holding my left eye, scared to death it was going to fall out. My mom quickly put something on the eye, bandaged it, and the next day I was the talk of the neighborhood with a purple shiner the size of Texas. A couple of the neighborhood girls, the two McCall sisters from down Elm Street, showed up to fuss over me, and Pengra yelled down the street to T. B. he was never to step foot in that part of Seventh Street again.

In a few weeks, T. B. and his folks packed up and moved twenty-five miles away to Salem. Not because of Pengra's stern ultimatum, which at first I wanted to believe that it was, but because T. B.'s dad got a better job offer.

That encounter with T. B., and another one with a kid named Boyd from the central part of town, were the only two real fights I ever had as a kid. Well, the one with T. B. was actually only a one-punch, one-sided quickie, while the scuffle with Boyd was a bloody nose draw broken up by his cute sister. We later became very good friends in high school.

I mean Boyd and me.

Chapter 3

Our fearless leader Bob Pengra on bike patrol. Notice the no fenders. The Law of Mom quickly overruled this fad.

In showbiz with my Charlie McCarthy doll. It didn't last because they said I wasn't funny and you could see my lips move.

The old courthouse. Wherever you were when it struck five meant get on your bike and get home because it was almost suppertime

West Seventh Street. Where some classic touch-tackle football games took place, including a series of long summer evening Kick the Can events.

CHAPTER 4

THE CALLY *The classic swimming hole that defied certain death, the naked standoff against a giggling Indian tribe, the invasion of the dreaded East Enders, and peace in our time.*

I grew up with a swimming hole that Mark Twain couldn't have designed any better. It was located on a short stretch of the Calapooia River that ran near the west end of the town next to the city cemetery below a seldom used railroad track. Some ancient kid nicknamed the site the Cally, but most of the survivors remember it as The Old Muddy, the Slaughterhouse Stream, or Ole' Typhoid. I must add here, and I shudder to do so, that the Cally was located about a half mile downstream from the city slaughterhouse. Seeing a sheep's carcass float by now and then was a common sight. It's a wonder we all didn't die overnight from the plague.

To get to the Cally, we usually gathered together on our bikes on Seventh Street around one o'clock. From there we wheeled about three blocks west on Seventh to the entrance of the cemetery, went a short distance to the maintenance shed, dropped the bikes, walked passed some blackberry bushes, and then hiked up an incline to the railroad track.

At this point, the trail drops down on the other side among heavy brush and winds almost straight down over a hidden wire fence, onto a shady open space among some old trees. Then straight ahead about twenty feet, you'll find yourself standing at the top of a twenty-foot cliff overlooking the lazy Cally. To your right are some rapids and downstream a few yards it's a little calmer, but usually filled with driftwood. This area was never used for swimming or even skipping rocks.

To our left, about thirty feet pass some trees, is the Cally. It's located a little higher above the river here, but someone in years gone by was ingenious in their effort to make it easier for the rest of us to reach the ledge below that stretched along the river's edge for about fifty feet. Steps were carved in a safe zigzag pattern into the side of the hard dirt about twenty feet above the ledge.

But the focal point of the swimming hole was the ring. Tied to a limb of a tree that curved out over the water was a long chain and metal ring. Here a daring participant, like I was first at age eleven, would station himself on a small, narrow, wooden platform about a foot down from the top of the ledge, grab the metal ring, say a short prayer, and then push himself out and away from the tree. The key to one's safety here, which I learned from my first effort, is getting just the right amount of oomph to clear the tree. Once this has been accomplished, and you missed splattering yourself all over the side of the tree, you are then sailing high out over the still, muddy brown Cally. At the height of this exhilarating maneuver you let go, hold your nose, and shut your eyes. Once again you need to come up with another short but more convincing prayer just before hitting the water and tangling with the alligators you were convinced lurked just beneath its murky surface.

It should be noted, that back in the late 1930s, this area was regarded as the main Cally's swimming hole. Up the river another seventy-five yards or so, among some brush and short trees, was another Cally site. This area, which had its own entrance from another part of the cemetery, was for the more blanket-type, family-style swimming and wading.

Our Cally was for guys only, and we had our own swimwear code. Which was wearing nothing. I had been told it had been a long-standing code for that special part of the Cally as far back as the '20s. That is until one warm summer day in 1939.

Swimming nude at the Cally involved mostly hanging on to the ring, sailing high out over the river, and dropping into the water below, either in a swan dive, a pile-driver, or flip. You did it nude and that was the unwritten law of the Cally. No matter what you did, and how often it hurt. But you were one of the guys and you didn't dare whimper in front of the others. So what if it made you a tenor.

One afternoon, we were all going off the ring in single file, naked as the day we were born, whooping and hollering, when one of us, I think it was McClain, noticed some rustling in the thick underbrush directly across the river from the ring. Quick investigation from three of the older guys flushed out six girls racing in all directions to get on bikes and disappearing up a back road into a wooded area. Their identities were eventually discovered, and Pengra, our fearless leader, made a promise to someone in the girly group that their parents would never know. Of course, it would all be revealed some fifty years later at a high school reunion much to the amusement of their kids.

But our naked days at the Cally were numbered.

Located across from Central School was a large Catholic church, which also housed St. Mary's Academy, a school that was home to a contingent of American Indian children. During the days of the summer months, two nuns would line these little kids up on the sidewalk outside of the academy and march them, two by two, up through the west end of town to the Cally swimming hole. I mean the nice family-type Cally above ours with its separate entrance to the river from the cemetery. No problem.

That is not until one day the cemetery guys closed up that entrance for some sort of summer maintenance. The families then established a new entrance to their swimming hole a block farther up the river, but for some reason the nuns and their little tribe wouldn't use it.

You guessed it. They took the entrance to our Cally to get to their regular swimming hole and that meant marching by us guys all naked swinging off the ring or standing around the campfire naked and drinking homemade root beer. And we weren't budging. We were standing our ground.

I can still see the routine. There would be a warning from one of us that the Indians, five and six year olds, were coming and most of the guys would gather around the fire as quickly as possible with not a stitch on. Then here they would come, not more than ten feet away. One nun in front, arms folded, looking straight ahead followed by about fifteen little kids, boys and girls, marching two by two, gawking, smiling, and not saying a word, as they were probably instructed to do, with a second nun bringing up the rear, staring straight ahead with arms folded in front. Not a word was said from either side, except for a faint giggle here and there from the little parade passing by. As I remember, this went on for about four or five days. Then one afternoon, a group of us were standing around the fire, naked as usual, when a familiar policeman strolled into the scene. It was Perry Stellmacker, the Albany chief of police, no less. A hush fell over the setting. We're all going to the big house. I just knew it.

"How are you fellows doing this afternoon," the chief said with a friendly smile.

"Just fine, Chief." And then, "Okay, Mr. Stellmacker." Silence....

"Listen fellows," he went on, "from now on you got to wear suits, okay? You're inside the city limits and it's what you have to do. I can count on you, fellows. Right?"

"Right!" I think we all stammered at once.

The chief then turned and strolled away in the direction he came from. As I remember, nobody complained. A couple guys had their suits stashed in a sack and quickly put them on. Mine was home, but from that moment on, I never swam naked again, and neither did the others. I'll be darned if the coppers were going to throw me in the slammer for being naked.

Many years later, I asked the chief who was it that ratted on us and he said it was the Catholic priest himself who came to police headquarters to complain on behalf of the two nuns. He told me he had a tough time keeping from laughing when he confronted us half dozen naked kids standing around a fire. He said he tried to make the warning as short and stern as possible so he could get out of there fast without breaking up.

Then one summer day, when most of us were standing around the fire laughing about the funny Marx Brother's movie we had seen at the Granada, a lone stranger—a kid about fifteen—approached and asked how the water was that day. One of us mumbled an answer and the kid smiled, and without turning around motioned over his shoulder to someone behind him that everything was okay. And that someone was three of the toughest looking fifteen- to sixteen-year-olds I've ever seen.

The dreaded East Enders had arrived. The smiley one out front said his name was Jack Howard and that he and his pals were there to swim. We figured that, but it was the way he said it. Like if one of us had foolishly said, "No, you ain't" and that would be the cue for their hit squad to step forward. One of our replies was a life-saving smiley "Sure thing, fellas."

Within minutes, three of them were taking turns on the ring while the other two swam out to the raft and started doing their pile-divers off the sides. The rest of us just stood around the fire, gawking and not saying a word. We all knew what had happened. They had moved in and were taking over.

We got dressed, took the trail up to the cemetery, got on our bikes and rode up to Seventh Street and plopped ourselves on the curb in front of Ewing's house. The Cally had been invaded by the enemy from the East End and we were on the verge of surrendering.

For about a week most of us went back to the Cally but it was never the same. We had not actually been excluded, but then we weren't included. They controlled the ring and the raft and we could use them only when they were finished. The same with the fire. After they were done crowding around it, and left to go home, then we could take our turn, but by then it was usually down to a pile of embers. Anyway, the courthouse bell would strike five o'clock and that meant the day was over and it was suppertime.

I remember clearly the afternoon it happened. A couple of us were getting off our bikes and leaning them up against the cemetery tool shed when a dark red Model A Ford pulled up. Out stepped Ewing's older brother Keith and his best friend Bruce Smelser, two of Albany High School's star football players. They asked us to follow them as they made their way down to the swimming hole. Once there, Keith and Bruce had us stand back as they walked over to Jack Howard and his group as they stood around the fire. Some quiet conversation followed, then the slight nodding of heads, followed by the slow departure of the east side group up the path and over the railroad tracks leading away from the Cally.

The siege was over.

What Keith and Bruce actually told those guys was never really revealed at the time. They would only say that they told the East Enders their time was up and for them to get out. It was about forty years later when one of the leaders of the East Enders told me what had actually happened that day.

Keith and Bruce only had to mention to Howard that Tuffy Logan had agreed to pull his East Enders out of control of the Cally. Make no mistake. Tuffy had clout and he could have stood his ground, but he backed away because he liked both Keith and Bruce. From then on, a few of the East Enders, including Tuffy and Howard, would take an occasional dip in the infested Cally under the new share-time peace agreement.

World War II had just been averted two years before the bombing of Pearl Harbor.

Chapter 4

Cemetery entrance off West Seventh Street.
Gateway to the Cally, a swimming hole made to order for Tom Sawyer and
Huckleberry Finn

The day I turned twelve, I posed for this
picture while the guys were swimming in
the Cally.
I never forgave my mom.

Bob Pengra, assuming the role
as our commander-in-chief. The
parents had complete trust in him.

CHAPTER 5

THE BIG SHOOT-OUT *Gunfire with a view from the park, Harry Anderson's historic walk-by, and three sneaky kids with tears in their eyes.*

Certainly one of the big events in a kid's life in a small town like Albany was the too-good-to-be-true incident right out of a 1930s gangster movie.

The big jailhouse shoot-out.

As I can recall, it occurred during the late 1930s, like around 1938. The jailhouse then was a small two-story box-type dwelling that stood on the south corner opposite the First Presbyterian Church up on Fourth Street. This was just before the current Linn County Courthouse was built in its place with Takena Park on the east side and now part of the courthouse grounds. The jail cells were located on the ground floor while the upstairs was home to the sheriff and his wife. Can you believe this?

It happened on an early summer evening when a prisoner tried his break. The sheriff and his wife made it down the stairs and outside before the prisoner did and this is where he became trapped. Deputies happened on the scene, then the state police, and gunfire soon erupted from their refuge in Takena Park across the street. Soon tear gas was being shot through the windows. The prisoner didn't have a chance, and the crowd that quickly formed from out of nowhere were all crouched down in the park hiding behind trees and benches. This was better than watching the band concerts.

Meanwhile, at the bus depot downtown a couple blocks away on Second Street, Harry Anderson, Pengra's stepdad, was getting off a Greyhound bus from a trip to Salem. He was going to walk home from there, which was just beyond Seventh Street, maybe eight to ten blocks up in the west end. As he approached all the commotion, and noticing people frantically taking cover in Takena Park, he caught a sharp pain in one of his legs and collapsed on the sidewalk a block away from the jail. He had been hit by a glancing bullet. It was about this time the police stormed the jail and the prisoner quickly surrendered, then handcuffed and hauled away from the scene.

The news of the big shoot-out had reached some of our guys that evening and they were on their bikes to the jailhouse, but it was roped off. All they could do was stand across the street in the park and stare. There was no radio station then but news traveled fast in those days by telephone and I remember riding my bike the next morning across the bridge into town and meeting Pengra and Bacon in front of the Presbyterian Church across from the jail.

The three of us, surprising undetected, walked across the street to the jailhouse and peered through the open door where two state policemen were talking with their backs to us. Pengra motioned to Bacon and me, and we quietly stepped inside and into the walled-off stairway leading up to the sheriff's living quarters. We were suddenly struck by a heavy wave of tear gas that almost turned us back. I recall sitting down on a stair and choking ready to surrender, but Pengra kept on going so I stumbled up behind him. Bacon was nowhere. I'm not making this up.

At the top of the stairs was daylight from the open doors to the rooms with their windows wide open. As we stumbled through the rooms I remember seeing a lot of furniture and curtains. Then a huge figure with a badge suddenly stood in front of us.

"Where in hell did you kids come from?" it yelled. I don't recall either one of us answering, just only coughing and trying to wipe the stinging tears out of our eyes. Now I knew how Cagney felt trying to escape the big house. We were then led back down the stairs to the jail area, and there standing by the front door, staring at us wide-eyed was the sheriff himself and a state cop holding a tear-stained Bacon by the collar. Nothing was said as we were led out and finally told to go home. We reeked of tear gas fumes and when we each got home we had to strip off our clothes and take baths. None of us were grounded because each of our parents figured it was the fault of the police for letting us get as far as we did without being seen. Plus, the fact it was Pengra's stepdad, Harry Anderson, who who took a bullet in the leg during the exchange of gunfire.

Until the day Harry Anderson died, he continued to walk ten to fifteen blocks every day downtown to work in an office at Mountain States Power Company. His severe limp made him somewhat of a celebrity with us kids because he never tired being stopped along his daily journey to and from work to tell us about being shot during the big jailhouse shoot-out. Of course, much to the delight of us kids, his story became a little more embellished as time went by.

As for Pengra, Bacon, and myself? Among the guys, our popularity went up a notch or two. Even that cute older Shirley Porter a few blocks over smiled and waved to me once. She had never done that before. When school started in the fall at Hogtown, my teacher had me get up in front of the class and tell the story. I remember her frowning and getting that look when I got to the part how we helped catch the shooter by trapping him on the stairway.

I forgot her brother had been one of the police deputies on duty that day.

This was also during the time when a leading pastor at one of downtown churches was robbed at gunpoint in his office, tied up, and then robbed of his desktop safe. You have to remember these were the tough depression years, and for some, like this thief, was apparently in need of some beer money. I'll explain this in a moment.

A week or so after the robbery, McClain and I were exploring the brushy area down near Bryant's Park for some berries when I stumbled, literally, over a heavy large object. It was the safe. McClain made a quick search of it and pulled out some crumpled papers that identified it as belonging to the church. We quickly covered it with brush, got on our bikes and rode as fast we could up through the covered bridge that led down into the park, then down about four blocks to the police station on Second Street and through the door of City Hall to the desk of the Perry Stallmacker, the chief of police. McClain blurted we had found the stolen church safe.

We then got in the police car with the chief and his deputy and led them back to the park where we had covered the safe with brush. The chief said we'll be heroes for finding the safe and will probably receive a reward from the pastor. Plus, a write up in the local newspaper. Were we excited or what?

The pastor was called and he met us at the police station, which was only a couple blocks away. He was elated and said he couldn't thank us enough. There had been some money taken from the safe, but it was the documents he had stored in there that was worth far more to the church than what cash was taken. He said we deserved a "handsome" reward and you should have seen McClain and I light up like a couple of Christmas trees.

The pastor opened his billfold, which I noticed was stuffed with paper money, and handed McClain and me our *handsome* reward. One dollar each.

After we left the police station we never said a word to each other until we got on our bikes. I was stunned into disbelief, and I'm not going to tell you what McClain said as we pedaled away. If I did the publisher would cut it out anyway, or light a match to it.

The robber? No, he wasn't one of those East Enders. He was an out-of-towner and was captured a few days after McClain and I found the safe. He was sitting at a bar in one of those rowdy saloons on Main Street drinking beer and playing big shot by buying several rounds for those gathered around him.

Chapter 5

View from Takena Park toward the old courthouse on the left and the First Christian Church. Foreground is where the old jailhouse shoot-out occurred.

CHAPTER 6

NO-MANS-LAND *The world's longest trestle, the dreaded East End beyond Railroad Street, a reunion at the big house, and the kindhearted tough guy from the East End, and Russ the teenage flying ace.*

Earlier I mentioned that one of the forbidden boundaries during the 1930s to a kid from the west end of Albany was everything due east of Railroad Street. That's where slow-moving freight trains traveled from the main freight yards south of town through the midtown residential areas and then on to a forever-long trestle that spanned a wide spot on the Willamette River into the North Albany and Spring Hill farm country.

Let's stop here for a moment. It's a known fact that during this time in small-town America, local area railroad trestles attracted kids like a magnet. Why? Because they were there. We were warned to stay off them, not only by our parents but also by the tough-looking railroad guy. This trestle starting from the town side of the Willamette, crossed the river and continued on a slight semi- circle high above a lush green meadow bordered by the town's golf course. From here, it disappeared into a side of a hill covered with fir trees and then reappeared alongside Fairmont School on its way west to Corvallis and beyond. During that time, it was reported to be one of the longest railroad trestles of its kind in America. It still stands to this day.

While we're talking about the north Albany trestle, there were several stories reported down through the years of near mishaps on the structure. One was that a hand car being operated by two railroad workers derailed somehow and the two guys almost went over the side. Two Albany College students got trapped halfway across by an approaching freight train and had to take refuge huddled together on one of those narrow, rickety water barrel stands that jutted out from the tracks high above whatever was far below. That one made the daily newspaper. But word got around that the two collegians did it on purpose for the thrills, and that's what they got. They confessed they thought they were going to die.

Then there were a couple of our guys, Bacon and Dawson, who took a dare that they didn't have the nerve to walk the entire length of the trestle without getting scared of a locomotive baring down on them. They did it and then rode their bikes home followed by a railroad official who saw to it that their parents dished out the appropriate punishment.

My only encounter with the frightening structure would occur later in the spring of 1942 when all of North Albany, especially where I lived, was flooded. I was trapped in town and my only means of getting across the river and catching a boat ride home was walking the trestle. I did, along with many others that day. We reached the high ground on the north side then got in one of several motor boats operated by farmers in the area, especially the Holmes brothers. I caught one of those along with another passenger and made it to my flooded doorstep about two miles away. If I knew what was waiting for me I would have stayed trapped on the dry downtown side of the river.

When I told my ninety-two-year-old sister Julia I was going to write about the trestle experience, a look of horror swept across her face. She told me she walked it one time when she was in high school. I didn't know that. And I bet our folks didn't either.

For the next three days after the water went down, I was put to work cleaning mud off the basement ceiling, floor, and walls. Why I didn't die of typhoid I'll never know.

Flooding, or high water as we called it, was almost an annual occurrence until a flood control system was finally put into effect further up the Willamette River down by Eugene.

A moment ago I mentioned my sister Julia. When she was in high school during the late thirties, and I was her pesty little 13 year old brother, she had a boyfriend named Russ Sprague. He was fresh in from the Midwest with a particular pastime for a teenager you would never in your life believe was possible. He was a pilot. Like in airplanes.

The following is what would happen almost every Saturday morning. You could set your clock by it. One of us would stand as a lookout at the kitchen sink, staring out the window toward the filbert orchard until we saw a small speck appear in the distant sky moving south to north. The lookout, which was usually me, would sound the alarm that Russ was coming and anybody who was in the house at the time, most often Julia, my mom and me, would race through the kitchen and skid to a halt in front of the window. By this time the speck had made a turn to the left and taken the shape of a fast on-coming small airplane heading straight for the kitchen window. As it approached there would be a giggle or two, then a small scream and then suddenly a fast exit, or the sound of bodies dropping to the floor, as the aircraft peeled off and roared overhead. Then silence. The ace of the teenage pilots had struck again.

Russ Sprague's attack on the Merrill household, much to my exciting delight, happened many times, and I often wondered how he got away with it. I never remembered my folks ever saying anything. Russ once told me that he and a couple of local pilots flew their piper cub aircrafts up to Salem to pay a visit to their pilot friends at the airport there. A visit that turned into an air raid.

They bombed the Salem airport with over a hundred rolls of toilet paper. The pay-back game came a few days later when dozen of eggs were peppered down on the Albany runaway and hanger.

Going out on a date with my sister at the time was a challenge for Russ. I mean specifically getting out the door with her. Remember this was the late thirties and the big rage at the time, I mean all over the country, was the insane popular board game Monopoly. We had a card table set-up in the living room that was set up permanently for the game and there was usually two to four people involved in the on-going event. And that included Russ. When he would arrive to pick up Julie, he didn't stand a chance getting out the door with her for at least another hour or so.

A few years later, around the time the war broke out, Russ had become a test pilot for the Air Force, and one of the first aircraft he was assigned to test was something brought over from Russia. It would become known as a helicopter. One of his first solo flights, he remembers, was a noisy, frightening, vibrating mess that took him low over the New York skyline. The machine, which was hoped to be perfected enough to be involved in World War II didn't make it, but showed up just in time for the Korean War.

Just a few years ago I was standing on a street corner in Albany during the town's annual Veteran's Day Parade when Russ tapped me on the shoulder. What a great visit we had. He had become a mortician in Albany on the advice from a friend that this is where you can make a good living. He said when he started seeing most of his old friend pass through his place of business it was time to get out. When the parade had passed we said our goodbyes and went our separate ways.

Not too long after, my sister told me that Russ had died.

Getting back to Railroad Street and east to no-man's-land.

This is the wilderness where the tough kids lived. Madison grade school and junior high were only a few blocks away east of the Railroad Street boundary. We had heard it was common among these toughies to fight their way to school, in school, and on the way home after school. It was said you were a nobody in the east end unless your nose was broken at least once before you graduated. The joke among us guys in the west end was that if you went to school in no-man's- land, you would automatically graduate straight into the electric chair. To this day, and this is the truth, there are parts deep into the east end I've never been to. Keep in mind Albany back then had only about 6,000 people.

And what about the girls from the east end? This ought to tell you: I saw a girls' basketball game between Central Junior High and Madison Junior High played at Central that should have been called off five minutes after it started.

A foul was called on a Madison player and the girl with the infraction immediately took off chasing the referee around the court, yelling and punching him in the back. The frightened ref was a high school kid and was stunned with what was going on. This happened again later with a different east end girl who got to shoving the battered official. As I recall, the two girls weren't kicked out of the game, and the poor referee didn't have the nerve to call a foul on them. I don't remember who won, but you can probably figure who did.

Then many years later in the summer of 1946, when the war was over, I was playing semipro baseball for Albany and one of our early-season games was behind the walls of the state penitentiary north in Salem. The games there were played in a courtyard surrounded by a high wall with a guardhouse in one corner high above home plate. Out in deep center field is where the convicts gathered to watch the game. Behind them, and providing the background for left field, was a three-story factory building. If you hit this on the fly it was ruled as an automatic double.

After this particular game was over, three convicts from the centerfield crowd were escorted by two guards down to the infield where they shook hands with the Albany players. They were ex-East Enders paying their respects. It was like old home week. By this time the west end and east end had made peace among themselves.

One side note about playing baseball against the convicts behind prison walls. I played against them many times back in those days and in that particular setting there were many amusing moments that occurred, which were mostly orchestrated by the convicts themselves. This was one:

Family members of our players, who journeyed with the club for the novelty of watching the convicts play baseball behind prison walls, were allowed only up on the prison wall around the guard station above home plate. Keep in mind: even the umpires were cons.

During the middle of the game, the mother of one of our players who was at bat, didn't like a couple of the calls the plate umpire had called on her son. And she yelled down at him a couple of times to let him know of her displeasure. The ump, at this point in time, took off his mask, raised his arm to stop the game and slowly turned around to look up at the unhappy mother.

His dramatic pause brought a hush over the proceedings. He then addressed her just loud enough for all to hear.

"Look, lady, I'm not in here for being honest!"

I'm sure his reply was one of a number of stock answers he had created for the outside hecklers that would line the wall above him.

As the years passed, the East and West Enders, as they entered high school together, formed friendships that would last a lifetime. One in particular was Bob Jacobson, a short, tough sports-talented kid that you couldn't help but like. He took lip from no one, but his heart was generous and as big as the moon. Everybody called him Bobby Jake.

I need to take this time to tell you about an incident that was typical of Bobby Jake. Especially to a young fifteen-year-old like myself just entering high school in the fall of 1941. I was fortunate enough to make the varsity football team as a second-string sophomore half- back behind Bobby Jake. In the opening game of the season against Oregon City, Bobby Jake was hurt in the early minutes of the game. I got the nod to take his place. I weighed only 155 pounds, and as I nervously trotted on to the field, I heard our center Thad Looney remark to his teammates.

"Here comes little Merrill! If we don't protect him they're going to beat the tar out of him!"

Protect me they did. On the very next down my number was called and I scored on a 26-yard touchdown play. That moment was big for me, but it was what Bobby Jake did in the locker room at halftime that I'll never forget.

At the beginning of the game the starting four backfield players were issued flashy brand new blue satin pants. The second and third string backfield, which included me, were given a dyed-blue pair in a feeble attempt to match the satin of the first stringers. Coach Tommy Swanson had just finished his halftime pep talk when Bobby Jake took me aside before the team went back out on the field and handed me his blue satin football pants.

"Here, Merrill, I can't play the rest of the game, so I want you to wear these. You earned them."

Coach Swanson, who overheard him, walked over to us, smiled, and quietly told Bobby Jake to put the pants in his locker. I understood. Bobby Jake was the captain and those pants were his. His gesture would be typical of countless others that would affect so many people down through the years. Yeah, this was one of those bad tough guys who came from the dreaded East End.

I attended Bobby Jake's memorial service not long ago at a large church deep into the east side I had never seen before. There wasn't an empty seat in the place, and the room was filled up with friends from both sides of Railroad Street.

And I'm proud to say that I openly wept for my friend Bobby Jake.

Chapter 6

The trestle that went on forever over land and water and scared everybody crazy who challenged it.

Sister Julia during the summer of 1939. Ready for art school in Portland.

CHAPTER 7

COMING OF AGE *A whole lot of turkeys, going to the dogs with Lorrie, discovering the world of prejudice, and a born actor named Rufus.*

As I entered the ninth grade, or junior high school as more mature thirteen and fourteen year olds like to call it, you were now becoming more aware that girls weren't boys. Also during this era, it seemed like every guy you knew was named Bud.

There was Bud Fortier, Bud Spencer, Bud Moench, Bud Long, Bud Darrett, and at least two or three more I can't think of at the moment. That's just in Albany. In nearby Lebanon there was Bud Paige, Bud Cleland; and in Corvallis, Bud Harper and Bud Foster. I don't know why I brought this up except it was mostly during this time in life when this occurred. You hardly hear that name anymore.

One of my new friends during this time was Joe Rankin, who lived about six miles out of town in a large farming area. His family raised, among other farm animals, a bunch of turkeys that were kept penned up in a large open area a hundred yards or so away from the house. You need to keep this image in mind as you read on.

Being an inquisitive young, fourteen-year-old teenager, and a male at that, the blossoming era of girls and the mysterious world of sex was beginning to consume his curiosity. A fellow classmate by the name of Jack Layman became aware of this in their talks together during shop classes and decided to help Rankin. In his special way, that is.

For the price of $5, which was a staggering sum to a kid in 1940, Layman sold Rankin a small bottle of Spanish Fly. If the reader is unfamiliar with the term Spanish Fly it is what Viagra is today. I bet you can't guess where this is taking you.

When Rankin got home, he started to think about what he had done. He didn't trust Layman. Thinking that maybe what was in the bottle was not what it was supposed to be. He thought he better test it out first to make sure he wasn't being taken for a sucker. Now we can bring in the hundred turkeys.

Rankin took the bottle of suspicious fluid and went down among the turkeys at a good safe distance from his house where his mother was beginning to start supper. Here he chained one arm to a water pipe where the inquisitive turkeys began to slowly gather around him. His reasoning for this, he later told me, was that when he finished drinking part of the Spanish Fly with his free arm he then quickly tied this arm also to the pipe. This way both arms were now chained in place and secure enough so that he couldn't get loose. Meaning, he said, if the fluid was the real stuff he now wouldn't be able to run like mad up to the house and rape his mother. Honestly, I'm telling you the truth.

The bottle of Spanish Fly turned out to be olive oil and Layman, for the time being, was five bucks richer. That is until Rankin could get his hands on him. His mother was now safe and able to finish cooking supper.

Don't get up. This is nowhere near the end of the story. Rankin did such a good job chaining himself to the water pipe that he couldn't get loose and the turkeys were slowly closing in on him. The large menacing flock stopped just a yard short of their prey, all one hundred of them gobbling at the same time every couple of minutes. Rankin admitted that the noise, and especially their large threatening beaks only inches away, was a bit frightening until he was finally able to pry himself loose. He then made his way safely up to the house, and how he explained his wrist wounds to his mother he never told me. At least she was safe now.

It was during this time in the summer, shortly before entering Central Junior High, that I too had suddenly discovered girls weren't boys. I had fallen madly in love with a newcomer up from Eugene. Her name was Lorrie Landis, a cute outgoing Hispanic girl with a bubbling personality and an already adult figure that could stop traffic and get the horns blowing. Keep in mind that it was 1940 and prejudices were still in full bloom. But I wouldn't have cared if she was green. I was crazy for Lorrie. I was also fourteen, and she was also the first girl I had ever kissed.

Here goes. It was a warm summer evening and a bunch of us, including Lorrie, were up in the west end playing kick the can. When it was over, we all took off for home by either walking or riding our bikes. Just as I was leaving, Lorrie walked over, smiled, and then kissed me. I had a heart attack! I jumped on my bike, said so long, or something smooth like that, and since I lived in north Albany by then, I pedaled like crazy down through the midtown residential area, into the downtown business district, over the bridge, and into the north Albany area until I had to walk my bike up the driveway to the house. All of this as fast as I could.

Then it hit me. I didn't even walk Lorrie to her door, which was only ten yards away from where we played kick the can. The new expression for this kind of behavior at the time was "What a jerk!"

Soon school started and it was shortly afterward that I got up the nerve to ask her out to a movie. A quarter each to get in and a dime apiece for two cokes. My allowance took a hit but Lorrie was worth it. I then gave her a ride home on my bike and was rewarded again with another smooch. This was after I walked her to the door. Was I slick or what!?

The following Monday, I rode my bike into town as usual to go to school. After I parked the bike in a stall on the east side of the building I started my walk across the schoolyard to the door leading into the building. Up ahead of me about fifteen yards were four of the top girls from the ninth grade class slowly approaching, four across, in a stern and unsmiling manner. The only thing missing were the torches and pitchforks.

They stopped dead center in front me blocking any possible escape route. Puzzled, I offered a weak smile and mumbled an even weaker, "Hi, guys!" Then silence. Dorothy Mailer, the one in the middle with her arms crossed, finally broke the silence and spoke these endearing words.

"We just wanted to tell you that you're going to the dogs."

That was it. When they turned to go toward the school building one of them turned to me and said, "And you know what we're talking about."

At first I didn't get it until after I entered the school and went to my locker. Down the hall I saw Lorrie at her locker getting out some books and she looked for a moment in my direction. Her usual smile wasn't there. Just a slight raise of an eyebrow as she joined another classmate and headed toward a classroom.

Even at fourteen I knew what had happened. The message was that Lorrie was part "Mexican" and being her boyfriend was unacceptable.

I didn't back down, but the situation brought a sudden end to a possible faceoff I was prepared to carry out with the four girls when Lorrie, unexpectedly, moved away to Yakima, Washington, to live with her mother. It troubled me that this display of prejudice had sent her away.

Then in 1952, when Norma and I were standing on a corner in front of brother Frank's Men Store in Albany, watching the annual Fourth of July parade, there came a tap on my shoulder. It was Lorrie. She was in the area visiting some relatives and came downtown with them to watch the parade. She had grown into a beautiful woman, who Norma, standing on the other side of me, acknowledged with that half smile as she slowly turned to me. I had told her the story about Lorrie and my encounter with the fearsome foursome

When the parade ended, the three of us went across the street to have coffee and it didn't take long for the conversation to revert back to the 1940 schoolyard incident. Lorrie said the fearsome foursome had nothing to do with her abrupt move to Yakima. She was also embarrassed she never said goodbye to me.

During the war years, she married an officer in the army, and when it was over, they settled in with the allied occupational forces living the good life in a villa overlooking the Rhine River. I think she just thumbed her nose at the fearsome foursome.

But here's an interesting side note that didn't occur to me until years later. I think it was her mother who was Hispanic and her dad was a resident Oregon State police officer in charge of the local office in Albany out on the main highway. Her dad was known to the locals as Officer Landis and was well liked and a fair guy to everyone.

Norma remembers one time when she was just a senior in high school and was stopped by Officer Landis for driving a little too fast. She told him she was in hurry to get to a gas station before she ran out. Now there's a good one. Officer Landis drove to a nearby station, bought her a buck's worth of gas, and then drove back and put it in her tank. He then waved his finger at her and told her to not be in such a hurry next time. There was no ticket.

When I was "dating" Lorrie, he was separated from Lorrie's mother and lived with Lorrie and an older daughter not far from West Seventh Street. I can only recall seeing him a couple of times, and it was one of those times he told me he would often stop by and visit my dad in his office.

That was the only incident of racial prejudice that I ever encountered growing up in Albany. There may have been some, but I never saw it, let alone experienced it, except for that faceoff with those ninth-grade girls over Lorrie. I knew there were a few Jewish store owners and they were well-respected people in the community.

So was Rufus Bryant and his wife, the only two African Americans I remember living in Albany at the time. They operated a shoe shine parlor on Main Street next to the Venetian Theater. Today, at the Albany Regional Museum over on Second Street, their two shoe shine chairs and equipment are on display.

I need to stop here and tell one on Rufus. Back in the early 1950s, I was in an Albany Civic Theater play with Rufus titled *You Can't Take it With You*, an original Broadway hit and Academy Award winner (not because of us). It was about a rooming house full of colorful characters ran by Grandpa Vanderhoff. I think I was around twenty-five or twenty-six at the time, and believe it or not, I played the role of Grandpa. I guess I must have convinced some people in the audience because there were a couple who thought, because we had identical names, it was Pop playing the part.

Anyway, in the dressing rooms below the stage, the entire cast of about a dozen people before curtain time would be frantically getting into their makeup. A lot of commotion going on. And there would be Rufus, who played the rooming house servant, lounging on a chair, relaxing with a cigarette, and boasting he didn't have to worry about all that because he was already in makeup and ready to go up on stage.

For many years I couldn't walk by his place or go in for a shine without Rufus asking me when his Oscar was coming in the mail. He wanted to display it along with the picture on the wall of him and his friend Jack Dempsey taken during World War I.

Chapter 7

Central Junior High. The site where I faced the fearsome foursome head on.

CHAPTER 8

THE MOVE TO ANOTHER PLANET *A new life in Bib overalls, the unforgettable fenderless bicycle, and the long distance journey with the love of my life.*

In 1935, we moved to the country to North Albany, or to be more exact, near the Spring Hill area. To a ten-year-old kid who had spent his time being with the guys up on Seventh Street playing in epic touch tackle games and kick the can in front of Eastburn's house, this might as well be like being relocated to the moon. Actually, it was only about two miles across the bridge from downtown.

You take a quick right off the bridge onto Spring Hill Road and then go about one mile when you take the second right on to Nebergall Loop Road. Our house, which then was a tiny two-bedroom structure, sat perched on a little hill above the first curve you come to, all together, maybe two and a half miles from town. To me it felt like I had been deported and shipped to a foreign country. Then, thanks to Pop, he came up with a solution.

During the summer months I would pack a sack lunch and ride into town with him when he went to work. He then would drop me off in the west end in front of Ewing's house, and shortly after five o'clock he would pick me up and we would head for home. And then he even made it better for me.

On my tenth birthday in August that summer he took me to Baltimore's Bike Shop in town on Second Street and told me to pick out the bike I wanted. Was I standing at the gates of Heaven or what!? The shiny red one with the balloon tires was it. And I remember Pop paying Mr. Baltimore the outlandish sum of $30 for my new pal. Of course it was expensive. It was a World Bike. I was now ten years old and had my own transportation to and from the guys in the west end. Was I grown up now or what!?

What's interesting is that when Ewing saw me wheel up in front of him on that brand new bike, he wasted little time in approaching his grandfather and guardian, Mr. Hockensmith. Ewing was a year older than I was, and I remember him telling me he took his grandfather to a window and showed him how I was slowly riding around on my bike showing off for a couple neighborhood girls. The next morning Ewing was riding a new $30-light blue World Bike. Then within hours, after Cochran had pleaded tearfully with his grandfather, he too had a new World Bike. A red one like mine.

I can recall one weekend day in particular when most of us gathered in front of Ewing's house and lined up our bikes along the curb facing out toward the street. The roll call was Pengra, McClain, Ewing, Cochran, Dawson, the two Eastburns, Bacon, and myself. That made nine of us.

Then something occurred that even the slow moving car driven by Doc Wallace every afternoon at this time on his way to the hospital had to stop to see what was going on.

Pengra had removed both the front and back fenders from his bike and laid them on the lawn. He never said a word, but it was as if he had because one by one the rest of us took off our bike fenders and laid them on the lawn too. All eighteen of them. And you're asking why? Well, because it streamlined the appearance of the bike. Translated, that would mean, depending on which generation you're from, they now looked with it, classy, groovy, jazzy, cool, or hot. Take your pick. It was a fad at the time and our folks, on the other hand, warned us we would be unhappy with the strip down. What do parents know?

Then came the rain. By parent rule, all the fenders went back on after the dirty water from the streets and dirt roads splashed up on our backs from not having a back fender where it was originally intended to be. I mean phone calls were made amongst the moms. I remember the rule meant the bike doesn't leave the garage until all the fenders were in place. And they were. Never underestimate the power of group parenthood.

Having moved to the country, and now being something like three miles from the guys up on West Seventh Street, I felt my bike had saved my life. Once in a while, especially during the touch-tackle season, I would catch a ride into town and back with Pop but in the spring and summer months I rode the bike. It never left my side. That is, until one Saturday afternoon shortly before I turned sixteen.

I had leaned the bike up against the side of a Safeway Store to go in to buy a candy bar. I wasn't gone ten minutes. When I came back out my bike was gone. That quick. I reported the theft to the police but they could never come up with it. I never saw my bike again.

Before I leave the bike, there's one episode with it I should mention, and that means we need to move into the early part of my sophomore year in high school when I was fifteen. I wasn't old enough yet to buy my first car, so I still rode the bike now and then, but not to high school. After all, I was a grown up now. For the first couple of months, I hitched a ride to school with Pop until I bought my Model-A for $200 and got a temp license to drive it, but only to and from school. Not on dates. That wasn't going to happen until I was sixteen when I could get a regular license.

Here's the story. I met my future wife Norma the first day I stepped into journalism class, and, within minutes, she had accidently spilled a bottle of ink all over something I was writing. She was embarrassed and I was in love. I also need to add here she was a senior and one of the cute drum majorettes for the band.

After a hundred years had passed, I finally got up the nerve to ask her for a date and when she said yes, I went into a life-threatening coma. There was one other problem. She lived on a farm eight miles east of Albany. I'm now talking about what would finally amount to a thirty-eight-mile round trip. No Model A yet. And you guessed it. Just my bike.

Stay with me on this. On Valentine's Day in 1942, I rode that bike thirteen miles from my house to pick her up. Now, keep in mind, through a lot of the following, she's going to be perched on the handle bars.

I now pedal six miles back to town from her place to see *Lassie Come Home* at the Venetian, then six miles to take her back home, followed by the thirteen mile trip back to my house. There's your thirty-eight miles! Oh yes, it started to rain when I was pedaling her back out to her house, and it didn't stop until I finally got home, which was now something like 2:30 a.m. Soaking wet with a worried Mom and Pop waiting up for me by the fireplace in the kitchen.

What a jerk I was. After all that, I was still too bashful to get enough nerve to try and kiss her goodnight. Having gone through all that, maybe my bike just got up and disappeared on its own from Safeway that day.

It probably finally had enough.

Chapter 8

Our first home in the country before tearing it down and building a new two-story home with a balcony and three fireplaces.

CHAPTER 9

THE ANIMAL KINGDOM *Scotty, the alarm dog, the mysterious barn cats, the dog nobody could see eye to eye with, and Oscar, the patrol chicken.*

What family didn't have maybe a dog or a cat? We were no different, except maybe when we moved out into the country. In town I remember growing up from one collie dog to another and his name was always Scotty. And the special one that entered my life occurred on Easter Sunday in 1938. I was twelve years old.

We already had a Scotty when we moved to the country in 1935 and he was definitely a town dog. Several days before that Easter Sunday in '38, he went missing. I scoured the surrounding farm land, on foot and by bike, calling for him but nothing happened. Pop even ran a reward notice in the Albany Democrat Herald. Only one response.

On Easter morning, my mom answered a phone call from a farmer a few miles east of town in the Knox Butte area. A dog matching Scotty's description had showed up on his back porch and seemed to respond to that name. My brother Frank and I got into his car and went out to the farmer's house near Knox Butte, which was something like eight miles away. When we got there, the farmer brought the dog from his barn and immediately this collie ran directly toward us. He then turned and began jumping happily all over me and I can remember the farmer smiling and probably thinking the kid finally got his dog back. But Frank and I both knew this wasn't Scotty.

First off, he was a Collie/Shepherd mix and had a bob tail. Plus, a scar across his nose. It was a disappointment, but that only lasted for a couple of minutes. I had to have this dog, and Frank knew it. He used the farmer's phone and called home and Pop told him to pay the farmer the $10 reward money and bring the dog, whether it was the real Scotty or not.

From that day on he was Scotty. The kind of dog every kid dreamed about having. He answered to the name Scotty and I swear he understood the English language. We never trained him to do anything. You would tell him to leave the barn cats alone, and he would look you in the eye, cock his head to one side, and then sit in the driveway and stare at the barn. Wherever he came from, somebody had trained him good. When my mom went into the barn to collect the eggs from the chicken stalls, he would walk ahead of her, and if there were eggs there he would stop, peer into the stall, then look up at her as if to say "here you go." If there were none, he would keep on walking.

Scotty's sudden attachment to me was uncanny. This was no young dog. Maybe eight or nine years old, the hired man once told me. I often wondered where he came from and what his name was. Sometimes I would sit in front of him and call him every possible dog name I could think of. He would stare at me and not once did he react, only when I called him Scotty did he whine and start licking my face. As if to say that's my name now so get on with it.

Scotty's most enduring and entertaining contribution to the Merrill family life began, according to my mom's recollection, one midweek morning when she got no response from me when she stood at the foot of the living room stairs and kept calling my name to get up to go to school. Scotty sat at her side looking up at her and kept giving a quiet little whine until she finally looked down at him in frustration and told him to go get me up. To her astonishment, Scotty took off dashing up the stairs, skidding as he made the short one-step turn to the left at the top of the stairs, bounded on a dead-run through my open doorway, sliding across the bedroom linoleum floor, and becoming airborne before landing on top of me in bed. I didn't stand a chance. He was barking, licking my face, and trying to get under the covers. It was at first frightening but then it became hilarious. Except my mom now had a private weapon, and she would unmercifully use it whenever she felt the need, which became almost a daily morning routine.

That is until I outsmarted them both. Especially Scotty, the alarm dog.

I was awake in bed this one particular morning purposely waiting to hear Mom's dreadful faraway command that would spring her faithful alarm dog into action. It finally came. Then I could hear Scotty's panting and rapid pounding paws as he raced up the stairs. This was my cue.

I quickly slid out of bed and dashed across the room and into the closet. Just as I was closing the door behind me I heard the dog making that short turn at the top of the stairs before entering my room. Peeking through the crack in the closet door I saw him tearing across the linoleum floor and slipping as he went into his take-off for the top of the bed. Then I witnessed a rather startling moment.

Once he lit on all fours on the covers, he quickly froze in that position, just staring down at a rumpled pillow. I can still see him in that scene. I suddenly became overwhelmed with a sense of guilt. I had betrayed him in his morning duty.

I swung open the door and dropped to my knees laughing and calling his name. He jumped on top of me licking my face and barking like he usually did, but this time he was whining. And then he did something I had never seen him do before, even when we played outdoors together. He made a joyful quick complete turnaround, stood his ground from me and started barking louder than ever before. I swear this was meant for my mom downstairs, as if to say I was fooled for a minute but I finally got the little jerk up.

My mom used the dog alarm on me quite a few times, only now Scotty would slide up to the side of the bed and do his barking and licking the face routine. He would not jump on the bed to get at me. Mom and I would both marvel, even years later, that Scotty initially was only told once by her to race up the stairs and get me out of bed to go to school.

Then about four years later on a Saturday morning, Scotty couldn't be found anywhere. He never answered to any of us calling his name. I searched and knocked on a lot of doors throughout the neighboring farmhouses and nobody had seen a bobtail dog. This went on for about a week until I knew he was never coming back. It was like the time before. He had left one family and showed up at another in Knox Butte where I found him on that Easter Sunday morning.

Many years later after the war, I was remembering Scotty with Pop when he brought up something I had never known before. He told me Scotty was a type of dog that people, especially farmers, called a tramp dog. Every few years they would move on to another family. Then he revealed to me something he couldn't do when I was a kid.

Back in those days farmers had a right to shoot a dog if he was caught in with their sheep. It didn't matter whether they had killed any sheep or not, just being seen in among them gave the farmer the right to shoot in order to protect his sheep. But there was never any actual proof that this is what actually happened to Scotty. But I think Pop knew, but couldn't finally bring himself to tell me.

In the years following, before I went in the service, we had another Scotty that became very attached to Pop. He was a great dog, but it wasn't the same for me. By then I had entered my teens and had become involved in sports, plus having found Norma.

I want to mention there was another dog in our lives but he belonged to Billy Cochran when he lived with us for a year or two sometime before Scotty had disappeared. He was a large black and white whatever, Billy had named Lucky. The dog had a goofy fun-loving attitude who thought he was still a puppy even when he got bigger. Much to Billy's disappointment, Lucky's wacky personality became even more hilarious following a stick throwing incident in the filbert orchard. After which, you might say, we never saw eye to eye with Lucky again.

In his effort to teach Lucky some tricks, Billy started out by throwing sticks or balls for him to fetch and bring back. After a few tries Lucky caught on. I was with both Billy and his dog in the orchard when Billy threw a big stick about thirty yards down between two rows of trees. Lucky took off, picked up the stick in his mouth, and made a big sweeping, galloping turn to head back to his master when wham! He had slammed head first into a tree trunk. The stick flew one way and Lucky flew another landing on his back. He let out a little painful yelp and then laid motionless.

Billy and I looked at each other and then we ran to Lucky's side. The dog was out cold. After a quick trip with my mom to the vets, and an hour of treatment for the front of Lucky's battered head, we went home and Billy took over the responsibility of looking after the injured dog. In a couple of days, Lucky was back on his feet and was his old goofy self again, only now he had suddenly become, if it was at all possible, even far more goofier than before. Lucky was now cross-eyed. I mean like for good.

Trying to keep a straight face at the kitchen table was almost impossible. Billy, or any of us, would attempt to handfeed Lucky, and all the dog could do was look up at you with those big bloodshot crossed eyes waiting for you to guide the dog biscuit into his mouth. Pop one time had to leave the table and my mom would laugh so hard tears would stream down her face. I think it was sometime about then I slipped a pair of glasses on Lucky and he actually sat still without moving when Billy walked into the kitchen. That did it. Billy started crying. But what are you going to do when you got a cross-eyed dog looking up at you through a pair of glasses and slobbering all over the floor.

Lucky was later hit by a hop truck and died at the vets. Billy stayed on with us until shortly after Pearl Harbor when he ran away, lied about his age, and joined the navy.

Oh yes, we had the usual one or two house cats the dogs always gave a wide berth to when they came face to face. But in the barn, there was something like fifteen cats that never approached the house. The barn cats we called them. They fed off the mice, ignored the chickens, and you could never get close to them. You never wanted to anyway, but my mom would now and then slip them a bowl of milk or two. This was their domain and they kept it clean.

Last, but not least, was my mom's pride and joy: Oscar the Patrol Chicken. He was a big, beautiful, white strutting rooster that hung around and protected her while she worked in her flowers. I have no idea where he came from.

Scotty the alarm dog was on duty during Oscar's tenure, and he stayed clear of him and so did the cats. And whenever Oscar felt like it, he would chase you across the yard, which seemed like all the time. Only my mom could pick up Oscar, carry on a conversation with him, and stroke the back of his neck.

Something must have happened to Oscar after I left home because I never remember seeing him again.

I don't think we ever had him for Sunday dinner.

Chapter 9

Scotty the Alarm Dog on duty waiting for the signal to pounce into action.

My mom. Already to go into town, but Oscar is nowhere in sight.

CHAPTER 10

HOGTOWN *A new world of bib overalls, Annie over, snowballing the Southern Pacific, little Marvin and the snarling pirates, the cowboy daze and the day our lives changed.*

Ayear after my folks made the move to the country, I turned ten years old. It was a different world to me, and Pop knew it would be that's why he bought me the bike so I could stay in contact with all the guys up on West Seventh Street.

When I reported to the one-room country schoolhouse for the fifth grade, I didn't expect to be sitting next to Tom Sawyer and Huckleberry Finn. They were there, all right, and I remember that first day clearly. I wore a striped shirt, a dark dress-up pullover sweater, yellow corduroy pants, and new dark leather shoes. That wasn't the dress code for Fairmont School. Every boy in the room had on bib overalls and wore high-top shoes that I swore had cow manure stuck to them. Most of the girls had their hair in a bun, wore long plain dresses with an apron thing, and all wore identical laced up shoes.

Right then I wanted to get on my bike and pedal as fast I could up to west Seventh Street and enter Maple School across from Ewing's house.

I need to add here something very historically important.

Although the school was named Fairmont, it was called, especially among the surrounding farming community for more than fifty years up until this time, as Hogtown. This was because of one particular farmer, whose property bordered the school, didn't believe in the necessary expense of putting up a fence to keep his hogs from wandering all over the area. Especially on the grounds of the nearby Fairmont schoolyard. I would hear many stories about the hog invasions of Fairmont, some of which included their actual entry into the school.

On one such occasion, I was told a couple of snorting hogs held a school teacher hostage on top of her desk until she was rescued by a neighbor from across the road. Although fences were in place by the time I had arrived, the name Hogtown was already stuck in the minds of those living in the area, and that's included, of course, in the teasing vocabulary from the kids of the neighboring schools in North Albany, Oak Grove, and Fir Grove. Various name calling, all of which the publisher wouldn't let me list here.

The schoolroom alone would certainly have made Norman Rockwell proud. There was a big black pot-bellied stove to the left as you came in, and when it got fired up I swear you could hear the rumble and feel the heat clear into town. When it rained, we hung our wet, dirty coats on a wall next to the stove that would most always give off a lovely fragrance for all to enjoy. Along one wall were the windows and on the opposite wall hung a big pendulum clock, a picture or two of something I don't remember, and the back wall, behind the teacher and her desk, was the dreaded blackboard, which would be used for writing assignments, or as an area for confessing our sins in chalk fifty times or more for whatever punishment we had coming. Like laughing out loud and pointing at first grader Buddy Barnes for peeing in his pants again.

The major features of this single schoolroom were the desks. They were built to accommodate two kids at the same time and who were usually in the same grade. I shared one with Ray Widmer starting in the fifth grade. The desks were covered with deeply carved initials from past students and were said to be as old as the school, which I found out later, was built somewhere around the 1870s.

Across the back of the school was the woodshed, which also doubled for the school's favorite game: Annie Over. If you're not familiar with the rules, it went something like this:

After choosing up sides, and not always the equal number of boys and girls to a side, they would face off against each other, unseen on opposite sides of the woodshed. Whoever had the softball first would yell "Annie Over," throw it over the roof of the shed to the other side, and if it had been caught, the catching side would then sneak around either side of the shed, hopefully undetected, and chase the opposing side back around the other way. The object was to see how many the thrower could hit with the ball before the fleeing side could get around safely to the other side. The ones hit with the ball became captives and would then line up with the hitters.

When one side had them all, or most all, when the school bell rang ending the recess or the noon hour, they were then declared the winner. Understand? It really doesn't matter.

Our schoolyard was a patch of dirt only big enough for an infield to play softball on. Right field ended a few yards behind first base where a barbed wire fence was erected to keep goat with a bad attitude from wanting to play. Centerfield was wide open to the danger zone of passing cars, trucks, and an occasional team of horses, and left field was occupied by two towering fir trees just ten yards behind third base. The bases were usually paper sacks filled with rocks, except for the time when we were short a sack at second base and we grabbed Pauline Trecher's lunch pail for a replacement. I remember that didn't last long after her brother Bernard slid into the pail going for a double. Actually, he wasn't even at bat. He made the slide after running from a sitting position on a box behind home plate.

At first, I felt out of place because being at Hogtown was an altogether different environment from West Seventh Street. Some of the kids were from a religious background that didn't believe in certain social activities. The ones I do remember most was like not going to the movies, wearing specific clothing, and the eighth grade being the end of the line for their education. The boys, as well as the girls, were considered adult enough by then to stay home on the farm and work the fields. There was a strictness there I never knew, and I'm sure I must have appeared just as different to them. But their lifestyle didn't change the fact they were still kids. It wasn't long before we were all friends and some of my fun memories were those at Hogtown and being a buckaroo on weekends. Well, sort of.

What happened was is that I discovered Hugh Nelson's house at the end of the Nebergal Loop Road and started playing cowboy on the weekends. They had a riding academy where people from town would come out on Saturdays and Sundays to ride horses on their property that stretched about two miles through pastures and a wooded area along the Willamette River. Hugh was about three years behind me in Hogtown and we had become good friends, not just because of all the horses and saddles and barns of hay to jump into that made his place a kid's dream-come-true paradise. I was in school with him and thought he was fun long before he invited me down one Saturday morning to ride a horse. Was he kidding? I had no idea this wild west playground was almost in my backyard. I was on my bike and knocking on his door while he was still eating breakfast.

A stable hand saddled up a gentle gray mare for me and then swung me up on its back in one swift moment. He asked if I had ever ridden a horse before and when I told him about the time in second grade when I had that picture taken on a Shetland pony he just laughed and said that didn't count. He rode along with us that morning telling me that to do and not to do and by the time we got back to the stables I felt like an old cowhand. I noticed Hugh was good at it, and he was only nine years old. An added fun thing was I never had to pay anything and Hugh's mom always packed us a sack lunch of lettuce and mayonnaise sandwiches before we rode off on the range. But nobody told me about saddle sores.

After a few weekends I became quite confident in the handling of a horse, and it was then that Hugh introduced me to the unbelievable. Climbing into a pen and getting aboard a bucking steer. Actually, they were calfs, but they were still hard to stay on. After a couple of days of being slammed repeatedly into, and over the corral fence, and unable to even get on my bike to pedal home, my folks figured it was time I retired from being a cowboy. But not until I had my last ride into the sunset.

It happened on a cloudy Sunday morning when Hugh and I rode off down near the river. About half a mile away we came to a gate fence when Hugh started to get off his horse to open it for us. I told him to stay on his horse and I would lean over and unlatch it like I had many times before.

Lights out Zeddy!

My horse suddenly bolted to my left and raced toward a large tree limb that my raised left arm slammed into and threw me backwards over the horse onto the ground. The next thing I remember was Hugh standing over me yelling my name and I was hurting all over. Especially on my bloody left hand.

With Hugh's help, I was able to stagger up to the stables with both our horses quietly walking behind us. Once there, a call went to my mom and she soon had me in town to Doc Howells. I had several bruises on my arm, and nothing was broken. But my left hand was a mess. All my fingernails, except for the thumb, had been scraped off and two of my fingers broken at the knuckles. Finally, my cowboy and rodeo day were over.

The one good thing that came out of all this would occur many years later. I would tell my kids when they were little about my cowboy days and the injuries I got when riding the range. Of course I didn't tell them I was something like twelve at the time and I rode a bike to and from the stables. But I did tell them, much to their delight, about the lettuce and mayonnaise sandwiches Hugh's mom would supply our chuck wagon. You can guess what Norma had to start making them for lunch.

Then there was my 11th birthday. I wanted a party of guys to go see the movie *Slave Ship* with Wallace Berry and Mickey Rooney, so I invited my bunch from the west end and a few of the guys from Hogtown. I knew they wouldn't be allowed to go to the movie but maybe they could meet us afterward at the Elite Cafe for the usual cake and ice cream.

It was my mom's idea so she called their parents to see if they could attend this part of the party. "What have you got to lose," she told me.

When she got off the phone she said three of the moms gave their okays, plus their kids could also go to the movie. This was a stunning breakthrough. I still have no idea what my mom said and I was afraid to ask. The kids were ten and eleven years old and had never been in a theater before. Even at my age, I worried about the initial effect this might have on them. And when it went dark, I saw the look on little Marvin's face and knew a few moments later I shouldn't have worried. It wouldn't have done any good.

The huge screen suddenly lit up with the roaring image of the MGM lion in their faces, and a bolt of paralyzing, silent panic shot through their young bodies. This is the way one of them described that moment to me some fifty years later and the fear he felt when it first came on. And, of course, it didn't help matters any when the movie was all about snarling pirates, ships firing cannons at each other, and all of us kids sitting only three rows back from all the scary and noisy action.

Years later in high school when I was a senior, I was in the library supposedly studying when Marvin, then a a sophomore, came up and sat down next to me. Because of the age difference and the different classes we were in, we hardly spoke to each other. I also played sports and he didn't, so we each hung out with a much different crowd. It was a long way from Hogtown.

The ice cream and cake afterward at the Elite Café was something Marvin never forgot. But it was the movie, his very first one he had ever seen, that changed him for good. From then on he couldn't see enough movies or read enough books about pirates and buried treasures. Whenever a movie came to town based on this subject, he was given permission by his parents to go see it. Shortly after, I gave him two books I had on pirates and explorers.

Sixty years later, at an old timer's high school reunion, and knowing I would be there, Marvin walked up and handed me the books. One had been autographed by a supporting actor who had appeared in a movie based on one of the books. The actor had written: "To Zed, the mayor of Hogtown, thanks for introducing me to the movie pirates. Marvin, October 9, 1986."

That bit part movie actor had turned out to be Marvin. Marvin took off for Hollywood after the war, got married, entered the real estate business, and in his spare time worked as an extra in movies. Especially those that featured snarling pirates.

Those four years in that one-room schoolhouse turned out to be among the most memorable times of my life. The bib overall environment, the school teachers Miss Beight and Mrs. Warman, and all the fun kids, regardless of what they believed in when they went to church. And not once do I remember anybody ever throwing a punch. Snowballs thrown at train engineers and hobos in open-door boxcars, yes. It was in the rule book for kids.

Many, many years later the farm community surrounding Hogtown held a special event honoring the school. I drove down from Portland when I heard about it from an old classmate, and by this time I knew the old school had long disappeared and replaced by a modern-day structure.

A great many former students were there, but the only ones from my era were my first teacher Miss Beight, now Mrs. Paul (Sailor) Dawson, Tommy's older brother, and myself. They held a special tree planting ceremony in which Miss Beight and myself were the only ones involved. We were both pleasantly surprised. Just last week, I drove by the school and noticed the tree had really grown.

During all those years at Hogtown, I never really left the West End and all the guys up on Seventh Street. We played the same street games, swam at the same place in the dirty Cally, and followed the same routine on Saturdays of hanging out at the auction house, and catching a double feature up on First Street.

But changes were starting to happen.

The group of guys that were a little older than the one I was in were now in high school. Pengra was in that group, which included, among others, McClain, Tycer, Bacon, and Dawson. When I finally reached the steps of high school in the fall of 1941, one or two of these guys had already graduated or were seniors. That's when it dawned on me that I had always been the youngest of all the groups.

I had turned fifteen years old just a month before high school started. In the fall, I had become a member of the varsity football team and was one of two sophomores who made their letter. The other was Tom Cowgill, who had moved the year before from Lebanon. I also became a member of a popular boy's club, and during my first day in journalism class I met the love of my life, Norma Miller. Man, did I have rainbows in my pocket or what!?

Then one crisp, sunny Sunday morning the boy's club attended a service at the United Presbyterian Church. As we were leaving and slowly descending the steps to shake hands with the Pastor, Dawson's older brother Sailor had pulled up on a bike down front and started a conversation with one of the guys. You couldn't help but overhear him.

"Just heard on the radio the Japanese bombed Pearl Harbor."

I didn't hear the rest he had to say because the guy just in front of me turned to the one next to him and said, "Where's Pearl Harbor?" His answer was, "I think it's in Alaska." And I remember thinking to myself, *Yeah, that sounds about right.*

That moment in time was about to change the lives of every one of us standing on those church steps.

Chapter 10

With the love of my life, Norma, in front of her house after I finally got up the nerve to do this.

Hogtown. The class of 1937 with grades from 1 through 8. That's me in the second row next to the big guy on my right.

CHAPTER 11

THE ROAD BACK *Seventh Street revisited, the effects of World War II, a careful step into no man's land, and remembering the good times with G. T.*

As I started to write these final pages, I heard a familiar sound outside my apartment window. I adjusted the shades in front of my desk and for a few moments I couldn't believe what I was seeing. It was a scene right out of 1937.

Three kids playing touch football, or a reasonable adaptation. No, it wasn't West Seventh Street, it was the apartment complex parking lot. But it didn't make any difference. The kids' sounds and laughter were the same. Moments later I heard someone call to them and they were gone.

I wasn't dreaming. One of the groundskeepers told me the kids belonged to one of the crew and they were hanging out with their dad that day because it was spring break from school. I asked him if his kids ever played kick the can? He smiled, looked at one of the kids, and then turned back to me and said in all seriousness, "Kick your can?"

Obviously, he didn't have a clue what I was talking about.

Not long ago, I drove down to Albany to purposely go out to West Seventh Street and stand on the corner where Ewing lived. The only part of that stretch of street that had changed in nearly eighty years was the vacant lot west of Eastburns. There was now a small house there.

Of course, Clarence was no longer in a cage on a porch across from Ewings, but I swear I could almost hear that parrot whistle at me and screech, "Get a life, jerk!"

As I stood there at the quiet intersection of Seventh and Maple, which served as the east goal line for all those touch tackle epics, I couldn't help but smile as I thought about all the times Pop would pick me up at that very spot at five o'clock to take me home. The guys liked him because many times he would come early to load us in his car and go up to Numbskulls so he could buy us all a treat.

It was during those times he would make up little poems about each one of us. The two I remember were, "Ole Bill Ewing, always frettin' and a stewing" and "Little Tommy Tittle Mouse, lived in a little house." I wish I could remember all the others.

It was amazing. More than seventy years had passed and everything was just like it had been. Even the school signs were there, including the one that almost took my ear off. All the houses, which were old even back then, looked the same way and still in great condition. It was then I realized what had changed were the guys. The time following the Pearl Harbor attack saw to that.

Bob Pengra, the one that kept an eye on all of us, won an air medal as a tail gunner on a B-24 bomber that survived thirty-six missions over Europe. Jack Bacon was also a gunner, but on a navy dive bomber off an aircraft carrier in the Pacific. He was lost at sea and his mother never gave up hope that he would someday be found. Bruce Wallace was killed in a navy plane crash, while another, on a promise to a family member I wouldn't reveal his name, was shot down over Europe, escaped a German prison camp, and then captured again where he spent the rest of his time until the war ended.

Then one of the groups, whose name I'm also not going to mention because he still has family members living, had joined the navy and deserted just before he was to ship out to the Pacific. He was later caught and spent the rest of the war in a prison in Washington state. About fifty-five years after the war I heard he was alone in a senior living facility in eastern Oregon and was dying. I drove over to visit him only because of the memories we had of growing up on West Seventh Street. He died six weeks later.

Every one of the guys served in the armed forces during World War II. Ewing was in the US Army Air Force, Cockran was in the US Navy, and so was I as a signalman attached to a navy gun crew aboard a Liberty ship that made three trips into the Pacific. We were called the US Navy Armed Guard, and despite suffering one of the highest casualty rates of the war, very few people ever heard of us.

As I remember, we dropped anchor once off the Pacific Island of Guam for the merchant marine to deliver supplies to the US Army Air Force base there. Little did I know, until some time later after the war, that Ewing was stationed at that base. US navy guys, including those merchant marines from our ship, were invited to eat at their mess hall one noon with the army air force crews and the nurses from the base hospital. Ewing said he must have been there that day because he remembered about ten sailors sitting at several tables over. He said if I would have stood up and yelled if there was anybody interested in playing kick the can with the nurses, he would have known right off it had to be somebody from West Seventh Street.

As I stood on the curb in front of where Eastburns once lived, it came to me that George Tycer and I were the only ones still living. We saw each other at the recent Old Timer's high school reunion in Albany and he gave me his address where to send a copy of this book. He reminded me that I better have it in there that it was only he and I that didn't call each other by our names. I was Z. M. and he was G. T. How could I forget.

It started to rain so I got back in my car and drove more through the old neighborhood, then downtown, and back out toward the freeway to Portland. Norma would have loved to have been with me that particular day because she knew all the guys from the high school years. In fact, she dated three of them before I met her in high school. Dawson, Ewing, and Tycer (G. T.).

By this time I had lost Norma a few years back. She had spent more than five years in a memory care facility where she died peacefully. You never get over a loss like that.

I need to pause here and comment about the amazing effect Norma had on my life. As you know by now, she didn't enter it until I was fifteen years old and only a few days into my first year in high school. She was a senior (an older woman) and the only real girlfriend I ever had. We got married after I went in the navy, and when the war was over we raised five incredible children who grew into five equally incredible adults. They arrived in our lives in this order: Cindy, Sally, Libby, Zed Jr., and Tawny. I call them the Board of Directors.

And I need to whisper this: Since Norma came from a farm eight miles east of Albany, and attended Madison Junior High School where all those tough guys came from, I guess she has to be considered one of those East Enders. It didn't matter. I loved her anyway.

As I sat at a red light about a mile from entering the freeway going north to Portland, I was thinking back about the old times when suddenly something came over me. It was an urge to make a left turn and drive through the deep areas of the dreaded East End and into the places I had never been before. So what if Tuffy Logan was lurking in the shadows ready to leap out in front of my car to scare the you-know-what out of me. I was ready to take that chance.

After driving a couple of blocks, I passed the church where I had attended Bobby Jake's memorial service a couple years back. I couldn't help but think about what a kind guy he was. Then I drove a little deeper into a quiet residential area of treelined streets and made a turn on to another block when I came upon a playground of kids playing little league baseball. Not exactly West Seventh Street, but the same idea only now with uniforms, umpires, and parents sitting in a bleacher cheering them on.

I was parked along the curb watching the game for a few minutes when there was a rap on my passenger's side window. Oh crap! Those bad East End guys are here. I carefully rolled the window down.

"Sir, excuse me," a smiling bald-headed man in an Oregon Duck T-shirt said. "But are you who I think you are? We may have been in high school together." I knew who it was instantly. It was Ben Neeley, one of the East End toughies who was two years ahead of me and another one who had run off, lied about his age, and joined the army right after Pearl Harbor. After seventy years, I would recognize those droopy eye lids anywhere, especially that booming voice he even had when he was a kid.

He introduced me to his wife, Anna, who had been raised in Salem to the north, and then proudly pointed to two of their great-grandkids playing on one of the Little League teams. That's when I first noticed he had an artificial left arm from the elbow down. When he went to buy the three of us coffee at the snack bar, I told Anna I never knew that about him and wondered what had happened.

"He lost it in a neighbor's house fire about forty years ago when we lived in California," she told me. "He ran in and saved a little boy's life and got burned pretty bad on his left side. They had to amputate his arm."

When I got back to Portland, and later ran into Eddie Thomas, a former East Ender, I told him about seeing Bennie and his wife and the story about how he lost his arm. Eddie then told me how Bennie, ever since he was old enough to have a paper route, had always given away almost everything he earned to help others in need, often leaving packages of food on doorsteps without telling anybody. This included sending gifts to hospitalized children suffering from burns. Even Eddie didn't know this about Bennie until later in life.

How's that for another one of those mean guys from the dreaded East End?

There's at least another half dozen or so other guys east of Railroad Street that I knew who became some of the finest people you would ever want to meet. I first began to realize that when we all collided together in high school, a couple of them gave their lives during the war, which included two close pals who enlisted together and then were killed together in North Africa.

As I finish this page, the summer months are beginning to approach, meaning, God willing, I'll be able to attend another annual Old Timer's high school reunion in Albany. And close by, hopefully, I'll see G. T. sitting pretty much alone at the class of '42 table. I'll scoot a chair up again and we'll start laughing about the old days as one of the guys swinging on a ring and and diving into the dirty Calapooia River. Of course, we'll talk some more about going deep on West Seventh Street for one of Pengra's long passes, playing kick the can, and hiding with a bunch of giggling girls over behind Eastburn's house, and how we would race each other down the same street on our fenderless bikes through a muddy rainstorm. And then we'll both think of another hilarious saying we taught Clarence.

A short time later, I'll get up, give G. T. a big hug, and then get in my car and start the drive back to Portland. Like I've done many times before after one of these annual reunions, I'll start thinking back over the years about all those good times I had growing up in Albany.

And once again, especially this time in particular, I'll be thanking the Lord for all those colorful rainbows he put in my pocket.

Bob Pengra when he was a tail gunner on a B-24 with thirty-six missions over Europe

Home on leave with my sister Julia's daughter Linda, who would grow up to be a two-term mayor of Hood River, Oregon

My pop. The guys liked him because he made up limericks about each one of them.

All grown up sometime during the 1960s. L-R : Sister Julia, me, Mom, and brother Frank

Norma holding one of eighteen grandkids. Today, the number of great grandkids has grown beyond this and there's still no end in sight.

The board of directors: L-R, Tawny, Libby, Cindy, Zed Jr., and Sally. Doesn't get much better than this.

ACKNOWLEDGMENTS

First and foremost, I want to thank the wonderful family I was blessed to have in my life. My wife Norma, who started getting after me from the beginning to write down all these memories before I forgot them; and to my children, all five of them, who never seemed to tire hearing about all the fun things I did as a kid up on West Seventh Street. They are Cindy Hill, Sally Merrill, Libby Christensen, Zed Merrill, Jr., and Tawny Johnson,

A special nod to Cindy who traveled to Albany to take several of the photos for me.

Others who kept encouraging me, even when I would get sidelined on another book or film documentary, were these special people: my sister Julia Goode, Jim Johnston, Judith Starr, Ray Bradley, Doreen Danials, John McKay, Willie Brosseau, and Eric Douglas.

Then there are those at the Albany, Oregon Regional Museum, who kept reminding me that they were reserving a special place on their counter for this finished product.

And of course to my mom and pop who helped make it all happen in the first place, and to Norma and our family board of directors, who kept it going the rest of the way.

Printed in the United States
By Bookmasters